CLEANING UP
THE CHRISTIAN
VOCABULARY

Other Books by
VERNARD ELLER

Kierkegaard and Radical Discipleship
His End Up
The Promise
The Mad Morality
The Sex Manual for Puritans
In Place of Sacraments
King Jesus' Manual of Arms for the 'Armless
The Simple Life
The Most Revealing Book of the Bible

CLEANING UP THE CHRISTIAN VOCABULARY

Vernard Eller

THE BRETHREN PRESS, ELGIN, ILL.

Library of Congress Cataloging in Publication Data

Eller, Vernard.
    Cleaning up the Christian vocabulary.

    1. Theology—Terminology. I. Title.
BR96.5.E43   230′ .03   76-10984
ISBN 0-87178-153-0

To my FATHER and MOTHER
in commemoration of their
GOLDEN WEDDING ANNIVERSARY

Thanks
for all they have given me,
including my vocabulary—
Christian and otherwise

CONTENTS

7

CLEANING UP
THE CHRISTIAN
VOCABULARY

INTRODUCTION

Talk about a necessary evil!

That is precisely what we are undertaking to do: to make a careful examination of the words regularly used in categorizing different varieties of the Christian faith, differing emphases within that faith, different people who hold differing ideas regarding that faith.

Evil? Yes, indeed—although not because the words themselves are somehow evil, dirty, or wrong. Rather, it is the case that the people who use them are human beings and sinners (which comes to the same thing).

Thus, we sometimes use these words as a means of derogating and putting down other Christians—or as a means of patting ourselves on the back and claiming points over them. We use these words, too, to cloud the truth by over-simplifying situations that actually are quite complex; we rob the Christian tradition of its richness by organizing it into neat, narrow, excluding classifications. Finally, we hamper rather than help communication within the body of Christ

11

(and in the body's converse with the world) when we use terms that have no clearly understood meaning, where the speaker intends one thing and the hearer hears something quite different.

Yes, these words do very often have the effect of dividing and confusing; and to that extent, their use is pesky if not downright evil.

But *necessary?* Yes, this too. As imperfect as they are, these terms constitute the only means we have for thinking and speaking about the actuality of our situation in the body of Christ. The differences, the nuances, they are intended to treat *do* exist—they exist whether there ever were terms for identifying them or not.

For instance, what has become very obvious to me just by keeping my eyes open (and cinched by a visit to the Christian Booksellers Convention) is that there is a segment of the Christian church which really goes in for "star"-centered presentations of the gospel. That is to say, there is a concerted promotion of "name" personalities from the secular world (sports, popular music, the movies, politics, etc.) who are willing also to make a testimony for Christ. Now the sector of the church most active in this is also that which has most consistently identified itself as being "evangelical." An article in *Publishers Weekly* is explicit in citing facts and figures, naming publishers, titles, and markets that prove this to be so.

The sorts of questions, then, that should be faced are: How essentially is this phenomenon a part of evangelicalism? Does it betray anything about the nature of evangelicalism? Is the phenomenon itself a good thing or a bad thing? How biblical is it?

We do not propose at this point to answer or even discuss these questions but simply point out that they cannot as much as be raised unless one is willing to recognize that there are distinct groupings within the body of Christ and that some sort of terminology is necessary in identifying them.

The case is the same, of course, when we note that the theology of the death of God had its following exclusively among Christians who commonly have been identified as "liberals." Is that theology an inevitable consequence of liberalism? Does its appearance tell us anything about what liberalism is and how it develops? What does the theology of the death of God tell us about anything? Again, we are going to have to have a vocabulary of Christian groupings in order to as much as formulate the questions.

Now some people argue that none of the old distinctions have meaning any more, that we can drop all of these admittedly ill-used terms and proceed to speak as if all Christians were of a single heart, mind, and self-understanding. This, I would suggest, is wishful thinking of a most unrealistic sort—or else the thought of those whose own concept of Christianity is so broad and undifferentiating that they cannot accept it that the distinctions of faith are of vital importance to those who hold them. Thus it would be true, of course, that the debate between different doctrines of the inspiration of the Scriptures would seem trivial and unnecessary to one who does not believe that the Scriptures are inspired in any sense.

Certainly, it may be the case that the labels of our current terminology are misleading and that they spot our distinctions elsewhere from where they actually lie. Nevertheless, distinctions there are; and some sort of terminology for handling them is absolutely essential.

Differences within the church inevitably are aggravated rather than helped by trying to deny that they exist. Communication is essential if resolution is to take place. Thus, to cite just one example, the amelioration of racial conflict hardly is served by arguing that there are no differences worth mentioning between black people and white people. Communication, in such case, is rendered impossible, because there is no recognition of any gap to be communicated across and so nothing to communicate about. Communication can be stymied by refusing to recognize differences just as much as it can be by trying to make those differences absolute: "You can never understand me, because you aren't black!"

Just so, there is no hope that the body of Christ can grow in the grace and truth of the gospel entrusted to it, no hope of its making progress in the unity for which Christ prayed, except in becoming aware of our differences, clarifying them, defining them as accurately as possible, and dealing with them. In this interaction, weaknesses, deficiencies, and imbalances can be spotted and, let us hope, corrected. In the process, too, strengths and insights will be uncovered which can be shared with the wider body. The frank and honest facing of differences can contribute greatly to "the equipping of the saints for the work of service, to the building up of the body of Christ" (Ephesians 4:12). Yet all of this must assume communication within the body; and communication demands a vocabulary that can identify the communicators and their several messages.

The ideal, I suppose, would be to junk the old vocabulary, which has so much been used to confuse and divide, and start fresh with a totally new one that is precise, fair, objective, and accurate. Well, that's a nice idea, but it won't do!

For one thing, there is no guarantee that a new vocabulary would not quickly slip back into the distortions of the old one; the problem never has been with the words themselves but with the way they have been used.

For another, there is no one either competent or having the authority to determine such a vocabulary. Words gain currency and accumulate meaning only through their day-to-day usage by everyday people. And regarding the vocabulary we have in mind, certainly the people who use a given term in reference to themselves should have a major voice in deciding what the word is to mean. Even dictionaries ultimately can only reflect the general usage of a term rather than imposing a definition that the experts deem preferable. No artificially contrived vocabulary would help —no matter how beautifully laid out it might be—simply because, in any case, people will go on using the vocabulary they already know.

So, for better or for worse, we're stuck with what we've got (as, in my own case, my wife graciously has come to regard me). Consequently, the title of this book is quite literally correct: we are undertaking to "clean up" the Christian vocabulary rather than censoring it, pruning it, discarding it, or replacing it.

Regarding each term selected for treatment, we will look a little at where it comes from, what its derivation suggests it *should* mean, how it tends to be used and misused. Finally, we will give some suggestions on how it most helpfully could be used. In many cases it will become apparent that the word must continue to be used in a number of different senses; yet we can at least try for some clarity as to what meaning should be intended when.

We certainly claim no magic in being able to straighten out the language to the point that no confusion or division need ever happen again. Yet perhaps we can induce and introduce some considerations that will prove helpful in making that Christian vocabulary more serviceable and our use of it more true, enlightening, and edifying. That, at least, is the hope.

Admittedly, the book has a bias—as it would have, no matter who wrote it. Any writer is bound to do a fairer, more competent job on the terms referring to those groups where his own sympathy lies than with those identifying positions further from his own.

The bias of the present author definitely favors

the orthodox (which see), low-church (which see), sectarian (which see) tradition of radical (which see) discipleship (which, to see, you will have to look up in a regular dictionary). However, if, as is assuredly the case, a bias there must be, for the task at hand this one carries something of an advantage.

The more churchly (which see) traditions always have constituted a large majority within the body of Christ and thus have had a good press and carried the day in setting up our religious vocabulary, defining its meanings and implications. The so-called "sects" have had a hard time getting a word in edgewise.

My desire now is to be fair to all parties. But because I am who I am and believe as I do, I am likely to be fairer to some than to others. Yet, if so, I will be more fair to those who have been treated less fairly in the past. There will be nothing poetic about the book; and it may not even be justice; but I am going to do the best I know.

ADVENTIST (see Fundamentalist)

ANABAPTIST

Ana, Not *Anti*

"Anabaptist," in the first place, identifies a loosely connected group of Christian brotherhoods that arose in sixteenth-century Europe correlative to the Protestant Reformation. The Anabaptists clearly were Protestant rather than Catholic in their basic understanding of the faith, though, at the same time, they must be clearly differentiated from the mainline Protestant churches.

The most conspicuous—if not the most essential—distinction is that the churches immediately won the social acceptance and recognition by the state that made them legal entities, while the Anabaptists were literally outlaw Christians (and not the first believers to be so honored, it might be said). Anabaptism is thus an expression of the "sectarian" tradition (see "Sect").

The name "Anabaptist" was not freely chosen by the Anabaptists themselves but was imposed upon them by their enemies—in the very effort to make the outlaw status stick. The prefix "ana" (not "anti") means "again" or "re-"; so the Anabaptists were "rebaptizers." Their opponents in the state churches were concerned to establish the title, because they had uncovered an ancient church law decreeing that anyone who allows himself to be baptized a second time is liable to the death penalty. To tag Anabaptists with the label, then, was in effect a license to put them to the sword. In this instance, it might be noted, we have a Christian term used to *divide* a brother's head from his shoulders—although the more favored method of execution was death by drowning (baptizing a person to death, as it were).

Actually, the term was very unfair and misleading from the outset. The Anabaptists never made second baptism an article of their faith. They, too, held for just *one* baptism, differing from their persecutors only in specifying that it be one, *authentic* (i.e., biblical) baptism. To them, this meant that it must mark a deliberate, voluntary commitment on the part of the believer himself and thus could happen only after the person had reached an age when such commitment was a possibility. Even at that, the matter of a "second" baptism held only for the first generation of believers, occasioned by the fact that they, as infants, had been baptized into the Roman Catholic Church long before arriving at the Anabaptist conviction that only believers' baptism is biblical. Thereafter, of course, the regular pattern for their children would be to receive only the one baptism after they had reached the age of accountability.

That the label "Anabaptism" focuses on the issue of *baptism* is proper and accurate *if* believers' baptism is understood as being but the symbol of a much broader and more fundamental interpretation of faith. If, on the other hand, the term "Anabaptist" is taken to suggest that the crucial issue concerns merely the correct age for baptism, it is grossly inadequate.

The broader issue is perhaps best expressed in the term "radical discipleship" (see "Radical"). The fact that such discipleship *can* be undertaken only upon the basis of a deliberate, voluntary commitment made by a mature person is what makes the distinction between infant and believers' baptism symbolically appropriate. However, the discipleship emphasis itself denotes a following after Jesus, an allowing of one's life and walk to be so molded by him that it produces the fruits of discipleship: nonconformity to the world, Christian simplicity, an intimate sense of community, defenseless love (pacifism), self-giving service, the faithful martyr-witness, etc.

As a contemporary reference, the term "Anabaptist" should, of course, designate particularly those Christian bodies—such as the different Mennonite groups, the Amish, and the Hutterites—who can trace their ancestry directly to the sixteenth-century origins. However, it also seems proper that the term be allowed for some later-born bodies—such as the churches of the German Baptist Brethren family (Church of the Brethren), the Society of Brothers, etc.—that have been strongly influenced by the Anabaptists proper and that fully accept their emphasis on radical discipleship.

Historically it may be accurate that all contemporary practice of believers' baptism (including, thus, all the churches named "Baptist," those of the "Christian" [Campbellite] tradition, and others) can be traced to the influence of Reformation Anabaptism. Nevertheless, it does not seem wise to apply the term "Anabaptist" on the qualification of baptism alone but only as an indication of the broader emphasis on radical discipleship. The "believers' church" (which see) is coming to be accepted as the more inclusive term which covers both the Anabaptist and the other believer-baptizing churches as well.

Yet, define it as closely as we can, "Anabaptist" still is going to have (and probably *should* have) some fuzzy edges. For example, the Friends (Quakers) historically have shared many elements of radical discipleship even while espousing some theological positions that point in a quite different direction—and while not practicing any form of water baptism at all. Should they be called "Anabaptists"? And how about the "new evangelicals" (see "Evangelical") who are moving strongly toward radical discipleship and whom one observer has characterized as representing nothing other than a rediscovery of Anabaptism? Should they be called "Anabaptists" even while belonging to churches that practice infant baptism? If we do use the term in such connections as these, we will need to take pains that it communicates accurately; and my own feeling is that "sectarian" would be a better choice of terminology.

Finally, we need to note the existence of some more technical and less widely used terms that do infringe upon "Anabaptist" but which ought not be used as synonyms. Both the "radical reformation" and the "left-wing reformation" include and perhaps center upon the Anabaptists. However, they also include a number of peripheral groups that shared with the Anabaptists a radicality in standing out against society as religious outlaws but did not particularly focus this in a discipleship to Jesus as Lord and Savior. They belong with what we call the "cults" (which see).

ANTIDISESTABLISHMENTARIANISM

Wow!

We do not include this word because anyone needs to know what it means. In fact, it offers more exciting possibilities if one does not. It does, however, stand as a monument to what can be done with Christian vocabulary when one really tries. This word not only confuses and divides; it also *stupifies*. It can be used either to confound enemies or to impress friends.

BELIEVERS' CHURCH

Not That Others Aren't

The "believers' church" is a modern term that just now is getting established as the proper one to describe the phenomenon it identifies. It includes the Anabaptists (which see) but covers a broader territory to take in all those Christian groups that constitute church membership on the basis of the individual's voluntary and deliberate profession of faith rather than baptizing him as an infant. Historically, of course, the Anabaptists would form the core of this group; numerically, they are now vastly outnumbered by the many varieties of Baptists, Christians (Disciples), etc.

Believers' baptism is the conspicuous symbol of this type of Christianity; but even more essential to it may be the fact that these denominations came into being by breaking away from the state churches and so, at least originally, represented something of a dissent from culturally-established Christendom and a tension with the world.

The one danger against which use of this term must be guarded is in not allowing it to imply that the other churches do not include true Christian believers. That is not the idea at all; the distinction is merely that the believers' church is constituted as those who already are believers come together to form the church, whereas the other churches baptize unbelieving (incapable-of-believing) infants and then strive to make believers of them.

We should know that there have been two other terms in contention, although the "believers' church" is now largely accepted as preferable. (1) The "gathered church" suggests that believers are *gathered* to form the church, while the other churches take in whatever infants chance to come within their domain. (2) The "free church" was meant to identify churches that were *free* from the state and the ecclesiastical establishment; but this term was found to be so general that it could mean almost anything and so was very confusing.

As with other of our terms, the "believers' church" inevitably has some fuzzy edges. In this case, the Methodist bodies in particular, although retaining infant baptism from their Anglican background, were otherwise of such similar orientation with the believers' churches that at least some Methodists have shown a continuing affinity, interest, and relationship with them.

CATHOLIC

You Don't Have to Be Roman to Be Catholic

The word "catholic," in and of itself, means simply "general, broad, all-inclusive"; and the term properly can be used that way in any context, sacred or secular.

In the course of Christian history—at least up until A.D. 1054, when the Eastern church broke away from the West—although there was a considerable variety of faith and practice and some splinter groups that saw themselves as different, the Christian church was sufficiently under the control of one organization and hierarchy that it accurately could be called the one, *catholic* church. Thus modern Christians can repeat the Apostles' Creed, with its line: "I believe in the holy, catholic church," and mean by it what the original framers meant, namely, that they believe in that general, overall church which includes all who accept and follow the Lord Jesus.

Thus, too, it would be quite proper—although risky from the standpoint of communication—to use the phrase "catholic Christian" (with a small "c") to identify anyone whose conversation and practice indicates that he has a strong sense of belonging to the total church rather than just to an individual congregation or denomination (see "Ecumenical"). (And thus there arises the possibility that there may be Roman Catholic Christians who are not "catholic.")

Yet, after the denominations proliferated—particularly in the Protestant Reformation—some groups continued to identify themselves as the "Catholic" church. First in this regard is, of course, the Roman Catholic Church—although the use of the adjective "Roman," specifying that church which is headquartered in Rome, is as much as to admit that a distinction had to be made as to which *catholic* church one had in mind. Nevertheless, for a long time the Roman church did claim to be the one true church and thus the only *catholic* one. However, in recent years this idea seems to be giving way to the recognition that the church truly *catholic* is larger than any organizational body.

We need to be aware that, besides the Roman church, there are other denominations that have come out of the Catholic tradition and retain the word in their titles. There also are groups that do not use the word "Catholic" but *do* consider themselves the one, true, and thus in effect *catholic* church.

We probably ought to be able to use and to hear the word two ways, using the capital or small letter to help make the distinction. "Catholic" (with the capital "C") tends to mean "Roman

Catholic"—though we should remember that there are "Catholic" churches which do not recognize Rome and the pope. Small "c" "catholic" quite properly can be used in reference to the total church of Christ that transcends any and all organizational boundaries.

CHARISMATIC

Gifts or Wrappings?

The word "charismatic" is both a polarized and polarizing one—and thus a real bone of contention. Those who are hep on the word tend to use it as a designation of spiritual superiority; those who are down on it read it as a designation of freakishness. It should be possible to get the word defined so that it can communicate a little less heat and a little more light. At least we will work toward that end.

The term comes from the Greek *charisma,* identifying a divine favor or gift. We use the word in a purely secular sense in observing that such-and-such a person really has "charisma," namely, a natural quality of personal magnetism that irresistibly attracts people to him and gives him power over them. This usage need not concern us here.

The theological assumption behind the Christian use of "charismatic" is that the Holy Spirit (i.e., the presence of God showing itself in an intimate, personal, empowering, joy-producing way) can indwell a believer's life so as to bestow upon him certain gifts and bring certain fruits to bear in him.

In 1 Corinthians 12:4-11, Paul proposes a list of these "gifts": the utterance of wisdom, the utterance of knowledge, faith, healing, the working of miracles, prophecy, the ability to distinguish between spirits, various kinds of tongues, the interpretation of tongues. The list undoubtedly is meant as suggestive rather than exhaustive, because, a few verses later, while on the same theme, he adds such things as apostleship, teaching, helping, and administration. It is interesting to note that, in counterpart lists in Romans 12:6-8 and Ephesians 4:7, 11-13, Paul fails to mention "tongues" at all. Elsewhere (Galatians 5:22-23) Paul also lists the "fruit" of the Spirit: love, joy, peace, patience, kindness, goodness, faithfulness, gentleness, and self-control. And again, the list probably is meant to be suggestive rather than exhaustive.

Now, by rights, it would seem as though the term "charismatic" ought to identify any Christian of whom it can be said that God the Holy Spirit is at work in his life to manifest any combination of these gifts and fruits. Yet this is not at all the way the term actually comes to be used. Before we are done we will find it necessary to distinguish between two quite different types of "charismatics." Yet, customarily, the word itself carries a quite restricted meaning—which restrictions would seem to be three: (1) The individual must be one who uses—and uses prominently—a particular vocabulary concerning the Holy Spirit. To speak, for example, about God being at work in my life, or my desire to have him be in control, or the prayer that he might fill and use me, simply does not qualify. The language must be "baptism in the Spirit," "filled with the Spirit," "accepting the *full* gospel," etc.

(2) Likewise, the individual's *experience* of the Spirit also must follow a well-defined pattern. It must happen as a specific, datable event signalized by a particular emotional state and even pre-scribed behavioral manifestations. Nothing else qualifies as a *real* indwelling of the Holy Spirit, no matter how many of Paul's gifts and fruits subse-quently may appear in the person's life.

(3) Regarding the "gifts," then, that of speaking in tongues (glossolalia, ecstatic utterance that is partly or wholly unintelligible to hearers) is ac-corded a significance different from that granted to any of the other gifts or fruits Paul names. "Tongues" becomes the validation and guarantee of Spirit-baptism and thus of whatever other gifts and fruits may follow from it. Without "tongues," none of the rest can be credited as "the real thing."

We first presented the broadest-possible defini-tion of "charismatic" as including all Christians whose lives evidence the presence of the Spirit through any combination of what the Scriptures call "gifts" or "fruits." Every logical consideration would indicate that that is what, biblically speak-ing, the word *should* mean. Nevertheless, it is very evident that it never *will* be used that way. And it would not be very helpful if it were: it would identify too large a spectrum and not allow for the making of some necessary distinctions.

We next presented the narrowest-possible definition, because this is the one actually used (or at least implied) by the most enthusiastic and vocal partisans of the charismatic movement and also by their most passionate and vocal opponents. And it is easy to see why the term, used this way, inevitably will be a source of great discord and wrath within the body of Christ. The charismatics, in effect, claim to be a spiritual elite who take it upon themselves to disdain their Christian brethren whose lives may be as rich or richer in the biblical gifts and fruits but who lack "tongues" and the exalted state of consciousness. And from the side of the opponents, one can understand their accusation that the charismatics are misnamed, not actually focusing upon "gifts" at all but arguing as to whether the "wrappings" are correct.

However, the word "charismatic" dare not simply be left at that narrowest-possible definition, either—even though it does correctly describe a great many in the movement. Yet there are also many others whom it will not fit; we need to make a distinction for which we have no vocabulary.

I doubt whether it will turn out to be a contribution to the language but let me suggest the terms "balanced charismatics" and "obsessive charismatics." Both groups are characterized by the practice of glossolalia (and, whether or not it is right to let the implication stand that "gifts" automatically means "tongues," the word "charismatic" is beyond redemption in that regard). The "obsessives," then, are those who hold the narrow position described above. The "balanced," on the other hand, are much less restrictive regarding each of the three elements mentioned. They have spoken and do speak in tongues and have found it a gift of help and value. However, they do not make it *the* gift or the validator of all other gifts. They use it not to distinguish themselves from other Christians or to divide the body but to edify it. They are quick to recognize the variety of the Spirit's working and honor that presence in the lives of non-charismatics and in gifts other than their own. And finally, they keep their charismatic practice in balance with other aspects of the gospel, such as discipleship, social concern, Christian education, a listening to the total message of the Bible, and ethical living.

So, is "charismatic" a good word or a bad one? The problem is that we have only the one word, yet I feel a real necessity to use it two ways. For me, if the word intends the "obsessives," the implication is all negative—and painful, even, because of some personal experience with the type. But if the word intends the "balanced," the implication is positive—pleasant, even, because of some personal experience with that type. The word "charismatic" is one we will have to use, but one which always will need to be accompanied by some modifiers if our communication is to be fair, accurate, and helpful.

A few peripheral observations relating to the term also are in place. "Charismatic" probably ought to be used primarily in reference to the contemporary phenomenon, which is not completely synonymous with the older "Pentecostalism." A striking aspect of the modern movement is the way in which it has cut across denominational lines; it cannot be related to any particular denomination or even to any of the broader traditions with which we will deal. Although the obsessive charismatics show a marked affinity for fundamentalism (which see), and although the charismatic movement as a whole is probably more largely conservative than liberal, even these lines do not hold absolutely. For that matter, it is the very sector of the church that produces the most charismatics that also produces their most rabid opposition. The charismatic movement is a phenomenon in its own right, and it would be a mistake to try to tie it to any other.

Modern charismatics sometimes are identified as "Neo-Pentecostals" (the new Pentecostals), but it probably is wise to reserve the actual term "Pentecostal" for something different. It, then, refers to the earlier "tongues" tradition—which apparently was not the immediate source of the contemporary charismatic movement and which has shown no interest in getting merged into it. This earlier movement evolved into organized denominations centering upon the Spirit-experience and the practice of glossolalia. Some, though not all of them, bear the term "Pentecostal" in their titles.

In contrast to the broader and more open charismatic movement, then, the Pentecostals are denominationally organized (rather than forming loose fellowships within and across the lines of non-Pentecostal denominations), obsessive (as per the definition above), and as much as exclusively fundamentalist in theology. It probably is also true that they prize more dramatic and extreme physical expressions of Spirit-possession than most charismatics do.

CHRISTIAN (see Liberal)

CHURCHLY/THE CHURCHES

Not Every Church Is One

Here is another terminology that must be able to go two ways at once. It is bound to be confusing; but it also is necessary for saying what sometimes needs to be said. Used carefully, there is no reason it cannot be correct and helpful.

In everyday speech, of course, we use the word "church" to identify any continuing, organized grouping of Christians dedicated to the teaching and expression of the faith. Indeed, whether it is precisely accurate or not, we tend to use the word even in reference to non-Christian religious groups. Obviously, we will go on using "church" in this broad way, no matter what might be written here.

Nevertheless, we need also to be able to use the word (and particularly the adjective-adverb "churchly") in a much more restricted sense—yet without denying the validity of either usage. The "churches," now, signify the classic tradition of legal establishment and territorial comprehension, i.e., one church being officially recognized as *the* religious expression of a given geographical community. Although that tradition, as such, is gone, its churchly descendants still are characterized by being on generally friendly terms both with the state and the dominant culture. Also, these churches tend to be quite formal and highly-structured in worship, doctrine, and polity. And it is all these echoes of establishmentarianism that we have in mind as "churchliness."

The "sects" (which see), in contrast, came into being precisely in protest against and as a way of escaping these alignments. Yet it undoubtedly seems strange to identify the churchly type as "churches" when the sect type are called "churches" just as regularly. They have even incorporated the term into their titles: Church of the Brethren, The Mennonite Church, etc. Nevertheless, from the historical perspective it becomes obvious that the terminology does point to a significant distinction—and one that was very apparent at the time the "sects" were founded, when the participants saw what actually was at stake. Perhaps every one of the "sects" resisted the term "church" and sought some other nomenclature by which to identify itself: fraternity, society, assembly, brotherhood, community, or whatever. They knew they were not "churches" even if, in the course of time, the word "church" did come to take over the entire spectrum.

At present, there would seem to be no good reason for opening a battle between the churches that are and those that are not, trying to settle which are for real and which are for false. I'm not even suggesting that the non-churches which have taken the word into their titles should now move to eliminate it. Even so, it does seem crucial that each church know enough of its heritage to discover whether its origins were "churchly" or "anti-churchly" and thus be able to evaluate that heritage and make conscious decisions about perpetuating it.

CONSERVATIVE

Compared to What?

This word is a tough one—as confusing as any we will treat. Yet it is one that is very widely used and *will be* widely used. Let me suggest as a guiding principle that it is a valuable and essential term when used as a *comparative* but less than helpful when no standard of comparison is stated or implied. The counterpart to "conservative" is, of course, "liberal." We will use that term in our discussion here but also give it a treatment of its own (which see).

The conservative-liberal dichotomy, obviously, is used regarding many matters other than those of the Christian faith. We will not concern ourselves with these—except to make a couple of observations that affect the gamut. (1) It dare not be assumed that, because a person is conservative in one area or on one point, it follows that he will be so in all respects. Although, for many people, there may be correlation and a general pattern, such cannot be taken for granted. Consequently, it is dangerous to call a person "a conservative," as though that one category tells the whole truth about him.

(2) In almost any field, the course of time and the changing situation has the effect of sliding the conservative-liberal scale one way or another; it needs to be pegged in time and place if the speaker and hearer are to communicate. For example, in 1819, William Ellery Channing, as a leader of the nascent Unitarian movement, would, rightly have been considered a far-out liberal; but in the Unitarian movement of today, he would be considered very conservative. The frame of reference needs to be specified before Channing can be described one way or the other.

A "conservative," of course, is one whose tendency is to want to *conserve* the values, customs, and understandings that have come to us out of the past—this rather than habitually opting for something new. But even the most liberal of liberals will be eager to name a number of things he also would like to conserve; so "conservative" always must answer the question, "Compared to what?"

Yet even if we carefully limit our consideration to *Christian* conservatism, there is still room for the issues to get all confused. For instance, regarding our earlier distinction between the "churches" and the "sects," it is clear that the churches are the conservatives and the sects liberal, if not radical. Yet this ecclesiological distinction tells one nothing at all about *theological* conservatism and liberalism; the one categorization cuts right across the other. Just so, compared to the position of the church in general, pacifism would have to be called a liberal, if not radical, position. Yet many pacifists come to their belief from a very conservative theological and biblical base. Is such a person a conservative or a liberal?

Most often, in Christian conversation, my guess is that the conservative-liberal dichotomy is applied in three areas: theology (doctrine), moral behavior, and life-style. But even here there can be wide discrepancy. Indeed, it is almost common enough to be a pattern that conservative (even ultraconservative, fundamentalist) preachers and evangelists adopt a life-style of dress and consumption that is anything but conservative.

The upshot, then, is that, wherever possible, the term "conservative" should express a direct comparative in which the terms of comparison are clearly understood: "In this regard, So-and-So is more conservative than Whoever." "This congregation is more conservative than that one." "This denomination more than that." In this way we can make sense and describe something real; otherwise we are bound to create confusion and ask for trouble.

However, when the word "conservative" or "liberal" is used absolutely, without specifying the area of concern or naming the two elements of the comparison, the speaker most likely has *theology* in mind. Thus: "He is a conservative." "She is a liberal." Such statements, I would suggest, have validity only if the designated person or group stands well down toward one end of the spectrum or the other. Thus the statement actually intends:

41

"Theologically, she (or 'that church') is more conservative than the bulk of Christians or churches." "Theologically, he (or 'that church') is more liberal than the bulk of Christians or churches." This way of speaking, done carefully, also can make sense.

Notice, however, that this leaves a great group of both Christians and churches in the center who cannot be so treated. To call them either conservative or liberal would be to mislead. They are in the bulk and so can hardly be compared against the bulk; and other than the bulk, there is no accepted and well-defined line by which conservatives and liberals can be separated. The comparison *can* be made *within* the bulk when *two* entities are identified. For example, it probably could be said that, theologically, Presbyterians are generally more conservative than Methodists. But neither denomination, by itself, should be called either conservative or liberal; neither stands near enough an extreme to make possible a differentiation from the bulk. Interestingly, in converse, it also would undoubtedly be accurate to say, "This *particular* Methodist is more conservative than that *particular* Presbyterian." The difference between the two denominations is not great enough to give any assurance as to how two individual members would compare. However, one would hardly go wrong to say that *any* Southern Baptist is more conservative than *any* Unitarian; here we are getting closer to the extremes.

The assumption that every person—any person—can and even should be categorized as either a conservative or a liberal is, I feel, a very harmful one. Let me use myself as an example by way of making a point. Some people are happy to be called conservatives and are quick to identify themselves as such. God bless them (as long as they don't intend that to mean "Thank God that I am not as other men, namely, those darned liberals.") Some people are happy to be called liberals and are quick to identify themselves as such. God bless them, too (as long as they don't intend that to mean "Thank God that I am not as other men, namely, those know-nothing conservatives"). But me? I get very uptight to be called either one; and if I were forced to choose between one or the other, I honestly don't know which way I would go. I don't want to be as far toward either end of the spectrum as those terms inevitably put a person; and there is no neat line in the exact center from which one can position oneself.

It is not the case that I don't know where I stand or that I am reluctant to put forth my beliefs for public examination and evaluation. They are there, hanging out, en masse—in books, articles, lectures, sermons, interviews, and conversations. I don't mind at all someone's saying that, theologically, this particular book of Eller's is more conservative than this other book on the same subject; or that he tends to be more liberal than most evangelical scholars on this point; or that he is way out in left field in trying to make a biblical case for universal restoration—or a hidebound conservative in his stance on abortion. I am even willing to have people say (and will say it myself, to beat them to it) that, theologically, I am probably more conservative than most of the Church of the Brethren *leadership* (i.e., denominational officials, staff, and prominent pastors) but more liberal than most of the Church of the Brethren *laity*. Whether or not all such observations are absolutely correct, they do represent valid and proper ways of making judgments.

However, to call me either "a liberal" or "a conservative" is to do me an injustice. Most of my books, I know, are unacceptable both to right-wing conservatives (I engage in biblical criticism) and left-wing liberals (I give the Bible way too much authority). They are read by some people who stand with me, some who are somewhat more conservative than I am, and some who are somewhat more liberal. Some of these readers like what they read, and others do not—but that line does not form any sort of theological pattern that puts me into one category or the other. And my argument, of course, is meant to apply not to myself alone but to show that, although any person's thought can be analyzed according to conservative-liberal categories, there are a great many Christians who cannot justly be assigned to either group. The words "conservative" and "liberal" must be used with great care.

CULT

To Have a Cult Is Not to Be One

The word "cult" carries two distinct meanings within religious parlance. We will talk about the first only to keep it from getting confused with the second.

A group's "cult," in this case, designates the system of ritual, ceremony, and custom that forms its worship practice. Every church has its own. The ancient Hebrews had a cult of animal sacrifice which, in time, became a full-fledged temple cult. We seldom use the word in reference to modern church practice; but it would be correct to do so.

The second usage is the one that interests us here. A "cult," now, is a type of church. The word is particularly necessary to keep these churches from being counted in with the "sects," which they are not (see "Sect"). Customarily the sects have been sneered at and looked down upon for being small and different—which, we shall see, is hardly an adequate way of characterizing them. But because the cults also are small (in reputation if not in size) and even more extremely different, lumping the two together has made it easier to consign the whole batch into outer darkness.

There is, however, a very particular distinction between the two types, even though it may not always be easy to separate those that lie near the dividing line. In basic doctrine and practice, a sect is "orthodox" (which see) and a cult is "heterodox." "Orthodox" comes from Greek roots meaning *"correct* opinion, or thought"; "heterodox" means *"different,* or *divergent,* thought." Now, of course, to get an agreed-upon definition of Christian orthodoxy is a sticky business indeed; some churches would define it so closely that they and only they would qualify. For present purposes, however, we need do it only in rather loose and general terms. Orthodox Christianity, let us say, takes the Bible (and particularly the New Testament) as the basis of faith, accepts Jesus Christ as only Lord and Savior, and generally is in agreement with the longtime, overall tradition of what the church has established as basic doctrine. So understood, the sects fall within Christian orthodoxy.

The cults, then, either make no pretense of coming within those parameters or else would have trouble getting their claim recognized by the groups that clearly are in. One rough indicator is that the cults generally show no interest in joining councils of churches or any such cooperative endeavors. This is not to say that every group that declines to cooperate is a cult; some quite orthodox groups choose to go it alone. But the cults generally are aware that their "truth" is different and shouldn't even be tried to make fit with that of the orthodox.

The cults are too numerous to list; but some of the prominent ones are Sun Myung Moon's Unification Church, the Jehovah's Witnesses, Christian Science, the Church of the Latter-Day Saints, the Seventh Day Adventists. And there is a purpose behind my order of listing: it represents a closer and closer approach toward orthodoxy. The final test is whether the group demands, as a test of membrship, any beliefs or practices derived from sources other than those of Christian orthodoxy. If, for example, the Seventh Day Adventist Church gives definitive weight to the revelations of Sister Ellen White (whether regarding dietary practice or whatever), this would put it outside Christian orthodoxy.

The moral is that one ought to be sure he has thorough and reliable information before judging any group to be a "cult." Yet the most important consideration, we insist again, is that one understand the difference and not put the cults and the sects into the same basket.

DISPENSATIONALIST (see Fundamentalist)

ECUMENICAL

Truth Before Unity

The Greek root of "ecumenical" means "per-
taining to the whole inhabited world." Actually,
then, the meaning is very close to that of
"catholic," though "ecumenical" has the advantage
in never having been used in the title of a particular church. But an ecumenical Christian is one
whose activity and attitude manifests a sense of
belonging to the larger church, the total body of
Christ encompassing all Christians.

This is what the word *should* mean; in practice,
I am afraid, we have let it take on a more con-
stricted meaning. Most often we use it to designate
a person's support of and participation in the
organizational activities of a council of churches
or other interdenominational cooperative. It is
particularly unfortunate if we go on to identify
"ecumenical" solely with the National Council and
World Council of Churches.

Of course, the specific programs and emphases of the innumerable interdenominational and non-denominational agencies (covering the entire theological spectrum) each must be evaluated as to how well it conforms to the Christian gospel; none is justified simply on the grounds of its being "ecumenical." Nevertheless, all these organizational efforts can and do contribute to our getting "ecumenical," being aware of and identified with fellow Christians beyond the bounds of our own particular tradition.

At the same time, it must be recognized that "programmed ecumenicity from the top down" is only one way of getting ecumenical—and perhaps even a secondary one. The other way is "spontaneous fellowship from the bottom up," i.e., individual Christians and congregations simply discovering their commonality with other-type Christians and, consequently, sharing with them and doing things together. Of course, there is no contradiction at all between the "top-down" and "bottom-up" movements; they can and should feed into each other. But we are skewing the term if we let "ecumenicity" identify only large-scale organizational activity—and particularly if we call a person "ecumenical" only if he is involved at that level.

There is another misuse of "ecumenical" that is related. It dare not be assumed that only that ecumenicity is true which has as its goal the merging of the Christian churches into a single organization. Whether or not that would be a good thing to have happen is very much a matter for debate (and is being debated); it is an *open* question and should be left that way. But to imply that a person is more truly "ecumenical" *because* he advocates organic union is to bias the matter most unfairly.

The key consideration is that Christian unity can never be taken as a value in and of itself. The approach toward Christian *unity* can be seen as good only if it is, at the same time, a move toward Christian *truth.* The gospel claims, in the first place, to be a revelation of God's *truth,* the ultimate truth about man, the world, and reality itself; and thus the primary end and value of all Christian activity is in its clarifying, communicating, and witnessing to that truth. If, then, it should be the case that the churches, in the interests of Christian *unity,* were to decide that their various doctines regarding the nature of God were an obstruction but that they could get around it by agreeing to agree that God is dead, this might mark Christian *unity* (of a sort) but certainly not *Christian* unity; it would be a denial of what the gospel clearly presents as a central aspect of its truth. The question of truth always must take priority over the question of unity; and ecumenicity is of value only as an indication of our growth toward truth.

And this tells us something about the procedures and economy of getting "ecumenical." Obviously, the one reason we have differing Christian traditions, denominations, and groupings is that each body feels that it has an aspect of, an angle upon, the Christian truth that is not being adequately expressed through any other body. Indeed, the group sees this witness (and *should* see it) as a particular gift and calling from God, its very reason for being—*and that for the sake of the total body of Christ.* Paul, in fact, would suggest that we can be "members" of the body only *because* we have functions that vary and only as we *exercise* our variety.

Contrary to what some "ecumenists" would suggest, then, there is nothing unecumenical in any Christian's thinking that his own denomination is best, that is, the one nearest to the Christian truth—which is not at all the same thing as thinking that his has all the truth and the other denominations none. He *should* think of his church as best—while being entirely sympathetic that others should think of theirs the same way. Indeed, if he knows of a group nearer the truth, he would be under some obligation to get himself into it. (Both the nature and content of the biblical revelation clearly seem to disallow the view that there is no question of *the* Christian truth but only of personal preference, i.e., whatever idea is found satisfying and one is pleased to call "Christian" is as true as any other. That would make Christian unity either easy or impossible but entirely meaningless in any case.)

But true ecumenicity, it follows, does not proceed by a believer's backing off from his particular "truth" in order to facilitate "agreement." His ecumenical calling is, rather, in the company of diverse but fellow Christians, to make as clear and emphatic and winning a witness to his "particularity" as possible. At the same time, he should be as willing to listen and consider when it is the other fellow's turn to make his witness as he wanted that fellow to be when he was making his. To be "ecumenical" and to be "denominationally grounded" are not contradictories; the second, indeed, is prerequisite to the first if there is to be a functioning of the several "members" in the service of the one "body."

Out of this sort of interdenominational dialog there will come "truths" we can take from one another and the spotting of "errors" we can help correct in one another. And to be "ecumenical," then, is not the plotting of strategies and the devising of techniques that will bring about the structures of Christian *unity;* it is to be engaged in the search for Christian *truth* that will itself bring to light the unity that already is ours in Christ and which comes as a gift of his grace.

EVANGELICAL

Sticky But Good?

By all odds, "evangelical" is the stickiest word we will treat; "c-o-n-f-u-s-i-o-n" would be as good a spelling as any. At the same time, there is no word that more imperatively demands attention, because it identifies that sector of the Christian church where, for better or for worse, the action most currently is, and where some would say the future of American Christendom is most likely to be read. Yet the best we will be able to do is to trace something of the maze of the confusion.

The word itself can only be termed beautiful. It is based, of course, upon "evangel," the Greek equivalent of "good news," just as "gospel" is the Anglo-Saxon equivalent. An unkind presumption may be hidden if the word is meant to imply that "evangelicals" are the *only* Christians who have the gospel; but if the intention is, rather, that these are Christians who desire to be faithful to the gospel, the thought is nothing but good.

The word clearly has some correlation with "conservative" (which see) and "orthodox" (which

see) and involves some of the same problems of
definition and usage; but "evangelical" is even
more complex and carries some distinctive implications and overtones. It would be nice if one of
these were that the "good news" party demon-
strates more of Christian joy, grace, and love than
others do; but I doubt whether any real distinction
can be established on that score.

"Liberal," of course, will, in this case, again be
the "over-against" term, as it was with "conservative." One question that will need to be addressed
is whether "fundamentalist" (which see) is to be
understood as the ultraconservative wing within
"evangelicalism" or a separate and independent
phenomenon. I think there is a distinguishing
feature that makes the second alternative
preferable; but the important point is that fundamentalism dare not be used as a synonym for
evangelicalism; that would make for more confusion than is necessary and would be manifestly unfair to a great number of evangelicals.

Not too many years ago "evangelical" could
have been rather easily defined and with a good
degree of accuracy. The doctrine of the inspiration
of the Scriptures would have been the identifying
mark. Evangelicals were conservative Christians
who accepted the Bible as being inspired by God
in such a way that there was no possibility that the
original autographs included any sort of error in
any regard. "Infallible," "inerrant," "literal," and
"plenary" were the key terms. Of course, evangelicalism also incorporated many other doctrines
as well, but this matter of biblical inspiration was

the crux. The definition was clear and simple; the only difficulty was that it left an awful lot of orthodox Christians out in the cold, lumped together under the one obloquy, "liberal."

However, more recently there has surfaced a movement known as the "young evangelicals" or the "new evangelicalism." In itself, that did not have to be too upsetting. Their particular distinction was merely that they had come to understand the gospel as showing much greater concern over the social problems of mankind and demanding much greater involvement with them than the private-salvation emphasis of earlier evangelicalism had allowed. However, as chance (or Providence) would have it, the emergence of the new movement also had the effect of revealing some things that had been happening within evangelicalism as such, raising some new issues, and throwing everything into a cocked hat.

Quite by accident, I got caught in that cocked hat and, consequently, have decided that to recount the experience is probably my most effective way of describing the present situation. When it is "confusion" that is to be portrayed, I am not shy about recommending myself as a prime example.

Donald Bloesch of Dubuque Theological Seminary is a recognized authority on evangelicalism and is himself happy to be identified with the movement. In 1972, he published a journal article, "The New Evangelicalism," which later became the first chapter of his book, *The Evangelical Renaissance*—perhaps the first public notice of this current development within evangelicalism. In that article, he included quite a string of names of those he considered theological leaders of this new thing. Well down in the list appeared the name "Vernard Eller." I was incredulous but, as far as I know, am the only person who bears the name. Things got worse (or better, in the sense of "That's a *good* one!") when F. Dean Lueking, in reviewing Bloesch's book for a Lutheran journal, revised the list a bit: "By 'renascent evangelicalism' Bloesch has in mind people such as Vernard Eller, Donald G. Miller, Philip Watson, Elton Trueblood, Kenneth Hamilton, and Jacques Ellul." Further, when Bloesch and others list the theological notables who are considered progenitors of the movement, there appear the names: Kierkegaard, the Blumhardts, Barth, Bonhoeffer, C. S. Lewis, Ellul, and Malcolm Muggeridge—the very people I would name as my own favorites.

Yet none of those in the progenitor list would have subscribed to a doctrine of the plenary inspiration of Scripture. Of Lueking's list of renascent evangelicals, I am very sure regarding myself, quite certain of some of the others, and ready to venture that none of them take the position of inerrancy. And a biographical investigation of the men on both lists—church membership, schools attended, schools taught at, affiliations, etc.— would indicate that few if any of them honestly could be characterized as products (or even inhabitants) of the milieu which commonly is recognized as "evangelicalism." I immediately engaged Bloesch in correspondence to discover what in the world was going on.

I learned, first, that he uses the term "evangelical" in what I would consider more of a European sense than an American one. In Europe, the term "evangelical" has no implications regarding a literalistic interpretation of the Scriptures but denotes simply a general Christian orthodoxy as over against a "liberalism" that threatens to move theology off its biblical base. But this discrepancy between European and American definitions has opened the way for a weird one.

Karl Barth, acknowledged as the greatest theological mind of this century, wrote a book entitled *Evangelical Theology.* At that time, none of the Americans known as evangelicals would have given Barth or his book the time of day. He did not believe in the Bible (as infallible); he was a "liberal"; and his following in this country was entirely among seminaries that everyone knew to be liberal. Yet, today, Barth (dead almost ten years) suddenly has become the leader of a movement within "evangelicalism"—didn't he write a book entitled *Evangelical Theology?* No wonder the picture is blurred; somebody moved—and I don't think it was Barth!

Basic to the terminology Bloesch and his compeers are using, I am convinced, is the assumption that the two terms "evangelical" and "liberal" *must* abut each other and together cover the spectrum. Thus, whoever obviously is not a liberal rightfully should be called an evangelical. Bloesch even posed for me some of the issues that decide the matter: "One either accepts or denies the divine authority of Scripture over the authority of reason; Christ as the divine Savior over Christ as a great prophet. It is not possible to affirm the sovereignty and almightiness of God and also accept the presuppositions of the process theologians who remold God into the image of a finite, suffering companion. ... We must not only have compassion and openness but also be zealous for the truth once delivered to the saints."

I agree with him totally regarding the extreme cruciality of each of these issues and stand totally on his side of each one; but I can't agree that this automatically makes me an evangelical. As I told him, it won't do to use the European definition in the American setting; our word "evangelical" already has been too firmly fixed—and not only as a theological position but perhaps even more so as a cultural complex. For us, "evangelical" is spelled: National Association of Evangelicals (counterpart of the National Council of Churches); Zondervan, Moody, Revell, and Baker (publishers of evangelical books); C. F. Henry, Harold Ockenga, the late Edward John Carnell, and Billy Graham (evangelical spokesmen); Wheaton, Fuller, Asbury, Gordon-Conwell (evangelical colleges and seminaries); etc., etc.

I have no trouble at all with how Bloesch reads my work and where he places me theologically; yet it is the case that I got to where I am without ever having been influenced, hardly even contacted, and certainly not affiliated with that cultural complex commonly called "evangelical." I do, indeed, feel highly honored to be listed as a leader of the "new evangelicalism"—except that there is nothing *new* about the faith in which I stand (I was born into it; and my church, the Church of the Brethren, has been there for over two hundred fifty years) and it has never before rated as being "evangelicalism."

What is happening here, I think, is that American evangelicalism is opening out to admit a somewhat broader view of the Scriptures (along with a new social emphasis and perhaps some other things). Bloesch describes the position of many of the new evangelicals as being an acceptance of the Bible as infallible *in its message* (thus implying that it is not necessarily infallible regarding matters other than those concerning the way of salvation). I see this as being a rather awkward way of stating what the theologians of the progenitor list always have held in calling (and more importantly, *treating*) the Bible as authoritative, trustworthy, reliable. The difference is that the new evangelicals feel a need to retain the word "infallible," suggesting that their stand is closer to establishment evangelicalism than actually is the case.

These new evangelicals, then, *are* moving into what is new territory *for them.* Yet the fact is that there are many other Christians already in that territory who have been there all along—people whom the evangelicals earlier (wrongly) called "liberals" and who the new evangelicals now (still wrongly) want to call "evangelicals." There is a certain imperialism implied in this; and the harm I see in it is that it introduces an unnecessary obstruction to Christian fellowship. There are Christians from across a great many denominations who properly could be and would want to be part of this mix that is being identified as the "new evangelicalism" but who rightly feel no desire to be called "evangelicals" (any more than they would want to be called "liberals") and who resist the implication that they are part of or in any way in the debt of the evangelical establishment.

In point of fact, none of the distinctive emphases that identify the new evangelicalism has been derived out of evangelicalism itself—this indicated by the fact that none of the thinkers named as progenitors were ever anywhere close to the evangelical establishment. So, for example, some years before the new evangelicalism was even dreamed of, as the conclusion and upon the basis of my doctoral study of Kierkegaard, I sketched out the need for a configuration of faith to all purposes identical with what is now being called the "new evangelicalism" (even, I think, to the point of coining the phrase "radical discipleship"). However, I called mine "neo-sectarianism" (see "Sect"). As a name, obviously, it will never go anywhere; but it is vastly more accurate than "new evangelicalism" in spotting the true source of the current ideas. What I didn't come within a mile of guessing at the time is that it would be out of the evangelical wing of the church that such a program would win new support.

We have suggested that the appearance of the

new evangelicals has had the effect of putting the meaning of "evangelical" up for grabs; but that is only half the story—and half the confusion. Certainly Bloesch's analysis centers upon something real, something actually happening. Yet, when we let another recognized evangelical scholar get his voice in, Bloesch's picture gets contradictory and pulled all out of shape.

The man I have in mind is Francis Schaeffer, founder of L'Abri Fellowship in Switzerland and perhaps the most widely followed scholarly author and lecturer in contemporary evangelicalism. Schaeffer first became a problem for me when I read in one of his books that *Kierkegaard* is responsible for all that is wrong in modern theology. Quite apart from my personal offense, that statement, in itself, reveals a serious tension between Schaeffer and the new evangelicalism.

More recently, then, the International Congress on World Evangelization, held in Lausanne, Switzerland, was the largest, most important gathering of evangelicals probably ever to have taken place. Francis Schaeffer was a leading figure. I quote the *Los Angeles Times'* report of his address:

> "If evangelicals are to be evangelicals," Schaeffer said, "we must not compromise our views of Scripture. ... The issue is clear: Is the Bible true truth and infallible wherever it speaks, including history and the cosmos, or is it only in some sense revelational where it touches religious subjects?" Dr. Schaeffer, whose lecture was warmly applauded, called for a separation of those evangelicals who hold the inerrant view from those who do not. He said that the latter are not true evangelicals.

(I guess that answers the question of whether Don Bloesch should call me an evangelical or not.) In another connection, Schaeffer's wife Edith typified all views of the Scriptures other than her own as being "glucky black waste-oil." Further, at Lausanne, in the original draft of the congress "Covenant," as it came from committee, the statement on the Scriptures took a position that could have included the interpretation of the new evangelicals. However, under the leadership of and pressure from Francis Schaeffer, the final version, as voted, excludes anything except the strictest form of inerrancy. If anyone chooses to take that action seriously and follow up on it, the evangelical establishment has repudiated and disowned what Bloesch calls its "renaissance."

Again, at Lausanne, one of the featured speakers was to be Malcolm Muggeridge, British author, columnist, and TV personality, who has been named as one of the new-evangelical progenitors. There is no possible way in which Muggeridge could be called a "liberal"—except that, to my knowledge, he never has publicly stated that he accepts the literal inerrancy of the Bible. Nevertheless, although he later backed off, Schaeffer at one point threatened to walk out of the congress if Muggeridge was allowed to speak. Muggeridge did speak; and that speech later was featured as an article in *Christianity Today,* the most prominent and widely circulated journal of evangelicalism, where it was received with considerable acclaim.

How, then, are we to read Schaeffer? My own

inclination would be to categorize him as a "fundamentalist" (which see)—he shows all the proper markings—and thus consider him as outside of evangelicalism proper. But that won't work; the attention and deference given him clearly indicates that the evangelical establishment sees him more as its norm and representative than as an offshoot. But what then becomes totally incomprehensible is the discovery of the standing he has among *the new evangelicals*. He is nothing less than guru to the Inter-Varsity Fellowship, a group which obviously consists of "young evangelicals" and which lies, if not squarely within the new evangelicalism, at least, on the outskirts of it. More, *The Other Side* is one of the several periodicals that does stand most squarely in the center of the new evangelicalism (and perhaps even *defines* that center). It carried an interview with Francis Schaeffer and, as a subhead in oversize type, identified him as "the *dean* of *radically biblical evangelical theology.*"

Now I am used to being thrown into a cocked hat; but in this one I am completely lost. When new-evangelical Bloesch listed me, I understood him to be putting me on the faculty of "radically biblical evangelical theology," an appointment I was proud to accept. But if the new-evangelical *Other Side* is naming Schaeffer as *dean* of that faculty . . . well, obviously, one or the other of us needs to resign. And until the new evangelicals can decide who it should be, we are going to have problems—and no chance at all of determining what the word "evangelical" means.

Thus far we have been discussing only those complications of the term "evangelical" occasioned by Bloesch's discovery of a renaissance. But we aren't done yet; we still have to consider those complications occasioned by the fact that contemporary evangelicalism is also experiencing another renaissance. This one is larger, more prominent, and more powerful than the first—and (wouldn't you guess?) in contradiction to it. The new evangelicals of the first are very critical and even scornful of the second.

This second renaissance does not yet have a name, although we will propose one. Although it is not taking place on the intellectual level nor winning the support of the intellectual leaders of evangelicalism, it clearly is an evangelical phenomenon and an impressive one. None of the non-evangelical, or liberal, churches show anything to compare with it. What its *significance* may be, we will have to judge; but I propose that it be called "pop evangelicalism." It consists of at least four conspicuous elements which obviously are closely interrelated.

(1) The recent burgeoning of "Christian" or "Bible" bookstores, the number of "religious" titles they are marketing, and the sales figures for those titles are the talk of the publishing industry. (Best-selling books in the category now sell several times as many copies as they did just a few years ago.) The industry—quick to investigate—knows very definitely what lies behind this success. The books are by evangelical authors and are pitched to an evangelical audience. A very high percentage of

the *authors* are women; and just as high a percentage of the *readers* are—mostly homemakers. The books are not at all intellectually or theologically demanding. Their main thrust is to show how Christianity can give you whatever you need (or want) to make you *happy*. Happiness, here, is conceived very much in *worldly* terms. Become Christian in order to fit in comfortably with the world around you, to get the kinds of rewards the world seeks: success, psychological adjustment, popularity, sexual satisfaction, and goodness knows what all. Many of the books are biographical or autobiographical: "This is how Christianity did it for me; why not for you?"

(2) The evangelical church also goes in for "personality cult" in a way that the other churches do not. "Name" Christians are very conspicuous; and their names are promoted through advertising and media coverage, using the same techniques as are used regarding secular "stars." Some of these "names" are people—evangelists, preachers, healers—whose accomplishment, whose claim to fame, lies in their Christian activity. Many others are those who have made it in a secular field—sports, entertainment, beauty contests, business, government, the military—and who then append to this a Christian witness. These people are touted as being something special; and the implication is inevitable (not accidental) that there is some sort of direct correlation between being a Christian and being a darling of the world—or that it is somehow a recommendation of Christianity that the world's "important people" accept it.

(3) It is among the evangelicals that the "church-growth movement" really has taken hold. Here there is a deliberate effort to model the local church over a hard-selling business enterprise and go all out for "success" (again, in very much worldly terms): ever more and more customers, bigger and bigger plant, more and more professional-expert staff, splashy and splashier programming. Every conceivable gimmick is used to bring in the bodies—whether it bears any relation to the gospel or not: showmanship, public relations tactics, the big names, prizes, spectacle, entertainment, all the enticements of the world. The rationale, of course, is that any means of getting people in is legitimate as long as you give them the gospel once you've got them. No consideration is given to the possibility that the medium *is* the message—or at least "colors" the message. A gospel sold through "slick" procedures is bound to come out as a "slick" gospel rather than the scandal and foolishness of which the New Testament speaks. Yet, in this way, what it means to be "a great church" is shifted away from biblical categories and into worldly categories; and all the great churches of America are now evangelical.

(4) Our final point is illustrated from a newspaper report that appeared not long before Kathryn Kuhlman's final illness and death. It had been revealed that the "name" healer actually was a very wealthy woman who lived in very high style. A reporter asked her about this; and her response was, "When the Lord blesses, he really blesses!"

To be completely incognizant of what the New

Testament has to say about Christian simplicity and the spiritual evil of luxury and materialism is one thing. To justify that as being the work of God and a sign of his favor and blessing is something of a more frightening order. Yet the making of this sort of equivalence between Christian and worldly values—of whom Kuhlman is far from being the only guilty one—is something that is largely peculiar to evangelicals.

When I try to think of one term that will best characterize "pop evangelicalism" as a whole, the word that comes to me is "snazzy." (The word probably dates me; perhaps it should be "neat," or "cool"; but, for me, "snazzy" says it better.) Christianity now is presented by snazzy people ("names") through snazzy vehicles ("great churches," splashy telecasts, etc.) as snazzy possibilities for snazzy living (with "discipleship" an entirely forgotten note).

The difficulty, of course, is that "snazzy" is a totally *worldly* concept of which the gospel knows nothing and wants to know nothing. "God chose what is foolish in the world to shame the wise, God chose what is weak in the world to shame the strong, God chose what is low and despised in the world, even things that are not, to bring to nothing things that are, so that no human being might boast in the presence of God" (1 Corinthians 1:27-29).

I confess that I have not been able to figure out what it is (if anything) about evangelical theology that makes this sector of the church particularly susceptible to this form of worldliness. I do not understand why people who know their Bibles well enough to be alerted against other forms of worldliness (and liberals, it must be said, have their own favorite ways of going worldly) should be so blind concerning this one.

Yet the important thing to be said in this regard is that—although both "pop evangelicalism" and "new evangelicalism" currently are in renaissance—the one can no more be taken as the essence of "evangelicalism" than the other. It would be wrong, of course, to deny or forget the presence and influence of either—yet neither is essential to the concept "evangelicalism."

How, then, are we to use the term "evangelicalism"? Clearly (the only "clearly" in this entire discussion) the movement is in a state of flux—a sign of dynamic and life—moving in several different directions at once. But we can't simply suspend speech and vocabulary until things settle down and get themselves sorted out. Therefore, I am adopting the following guidelines for myself; you can do as you choose.

(1) I will use "evangelical" quite traditionally and narrowly, in reference to the culture-complex and theology of the evangelical establishment— that is, designating quite conservative Christians who move in circles known as "evangelical" and who hold a rather tight view of biblical inerrancy. (By this definition, I am *not* an evangelical.)

(2) Reluctantly, out of the exigencies of communication, I will call the "young/new evangelicals" what they choose to be called—even while maintaining my own reservations as to

whether what they represent accurately can be understood as standing within, being a variety of, or even being an expression of what has been known as "evangelicalism." (I *am* happy to be identified with this group.)

(3) I will be critical of "pop evangelicalism"; but I will not include that phenomenon as part of the definition of the word "evangelical" and so use it to put down the evangelical movement as a whole.

(4) Most of all, I will keep my perceptions open and listen very closely when anyone else uses the term "evangelical," doing my best to understand what *he* means by it.

FREE CHURCH (see Believers' Church)

FUNDAMENTALIST

Fundamentally Right

Almost anyone would agree that the fundamentalists stand solidly and fundamentally on the *right* end of the theological spectrum. Fundamentalists themselves also would be quick to say that, doctrinally, they are fundamentally *correct* in a way that other Christians are not. So the reader is free to take our title whichever way he sees fit.

The term "fundamentalist," of course, is meant to signify that the person holds to the *fundamental* doctrines of the Christian gospel. But because practically anyone who calls himself a Christian would want to make such a claim for himself, and because any person has as much right to make it as anyone else does, the term obviously cannot be defined by this method.

"Fundamentalist" plainly stands in close association with "evangelical" (which see)—a closeness which is much more profound than the alphabetical accident that puts them shoulder to shoulder in this book. Yet our most important task will be to establish a distinction that will prevent the two terms from being used as synonymous. Most evangelicals (rightly) would resist the label "fundamentalist"; and it would be an injustice to lump them together.

Although the roots of the fundamentalist movement go back into the nineteenth century, the name itself comes from a series of twelve tracts, called *The Fundamentals,* published between 1910 and 1915 and distributed to the tune of three million copies through the generosity of a pair of Christian laymen, Lyman and Milton Stewart. Although a reading of those tracts would give a good picture of the sort of things fundamentalists believe, the tracts themselves have passed into history and have no official standing as any sort of confession of faith.

One cannot define the term "evangelical" without using the concept "conservative" (which see); and it would be quite correct to designate "fundamentalist" as "ultraconservative." The only difficulty is that there is no neat and accurate way to draw a precise line between conservative and ultraconservative and thus make the distinction we are seeking.

There are a couple more terms that can be helpful in *understanding* fundamentalism, although they are not adequate to constitute a definition. The word "millenarianism" (or "millennialism") is based upon "millennium," a thousand-year period and specifically the one the book of Revelation mentions in connection with the end of this world and the second coming of Christ. However, "millenarian" is used somewhat more broadly than as a reference just to the millennium; it identifies the whole school of Christian thought that focuses strongly upon the events of the end, using the Bible to construct both a timetable and detailed scenario. "Adventist" is the term used by some churches for much the same viewpoint.

"Dispensationalism" signifies a specific and more refined style of millenarianism. It goes back to the work of J. N. Darby, one of the founders of the Plymouth Brethren movement in England; but its most notable expression is the Scofield Reference Bible. Out of this school of thought came the idea of "the rapture," a secret coming of Christ to take believers out of the world preceding his final and public coming at the end. Yet the most characteristic feature of dispensationalism is the charting of the whole of world history into different periods, or "dispensations," regarding each of which God has quite distinct purposes, actions, and directives. The all-important key in understanding and obeying the Scriptures, then, is to discover to which dispensation any given passage applies and to know in which one we currently are living.

Now a good many fundamentalists are millenarian and/or dispensationalist in faith. However, there are some who are not but who still should be qualified as fundamentalist; and conversely, there are some millenarianists and/or dispensationalists who probably should be called evangelical rather than fundamentalist.

I am ready to propose, then, that the ultimate distinction between "fundamentalist" and "evangelical" be made on the basis of *attitude* rather than *doctrine*. A "fundamentalist" thus becomes an ultraconservative believer who is completely self-confident that he is correct in his understanding of Christian doctrine, that only what he calls Christianity *is* Christianity. He then proceeds to bolster that sense of surety by expressing arrogance, belligerency, and condemnation toward any Christians (sic) who do not believe as he does. This attitude of dogmatism is what, for me, *defines* "fundamentalist."

I do not at all mean to suggest that this sort of intolerance is never found *except* at the ultraconservative end of the spectrum, but rather obviously it concentrates there. And please hear me very clearly when I say that I am *not* making any wholesale accusation that a group of Christians holding a particular doctrinal position invariably displays this attitude. I am *defining the term by* the attitude rather than the doctrine. Accordingly, because there is no line that can be drawn between conservative and ultraconservative, then, no matter how doctrinally conservative a person might be (millenarian, dispensationalist, biblical literalist, or what-all), I would call him "evangelical" rather than "fundamentalist"—unless he also displayed the attitude described.

Assuredly, there are any number of people who would call *themselves* "fundamentalists"— meaning that they consider themselves as holding to the fundamentals of Christianity—whom I would prefer to call "evangelicals." That is no problem as long as we let each other know what we mean by our terminology. Similarly, I would never call Francis Schaeffer (see the mention of him under "evangelical") a "fundamentalist" *simply on the basis of his view of biblical inerrancy.* I love and am loved by any number of Christian brethren who hold this view of the Bible but whom I would never dream of calling "fundamentalists." However, on the basis of his presuming to divide his evangelical colleagues into the "true" and the "false," and on the basis of his attitude toward Malcolm Muggeridge, I *would* categorize him a "fundamentalist." Yet notice, in this regard, that I use the term not so much to insult and reject *him* as to indicate my apprehension that *he* has insulted and rejected *me.*

Obviously, "fundamentalist" is a term to be used sparingly, with circumspection and care— and never as a synonym for "evangelical."

("Modernist" is a term that was brought into currency by the fundamentalists earlier in the century when their attitude was at a heat. It was used as a term of opprobium for anyone who held views more liberal than theirs. Today, the term "liberal" [which see] can be used to communicate anything that needs, or ought, to be communiated in that regard—and with considerably less venom. "Modernist" has been pretty well retired and should be completely so.)

GATHERED CHURCH
(see Believers' Church)

HERETICAL (see Orthodox)

HIGH CHURCH (see Liturgical)

HOLINESS CHURCHES

Wholly Holy

The "holiness churches" constitute a Christian movement that, theologically, stands close enough to "evangelicalism" (and on occasion "fundamentalism") to be confused with them—sometimes even getting *themselves* confused with them. Nonetheless, there is a distinction we ought to observe—and the holiness people ought to work at demonstrating.

Theologically, these Christians are conservative; but in addition they represent the Wesleyan tradition (i.e., they look to the teachings of John Wesley and his colleagues, the founders of Methodism) as it became invigorated and influenced by mid-nineteenth-century American revivalism. The most visible focus of the movement today is the Christian Holiness Association, to which some twenty denominations belong. Some of the more conservative members of the United Methodist Church probably should be counted among the holiness people; but the more typical churches are the Wesleyan Church, the Free Methodists, the Church of the Nazarene, and the Church of God (Anderson, Indiana). There are some holiness-Pentecostal groups (see "Charismatic") but most are non-charismatic and many are strongly anti-charismatic.

"Holiness" carries a particular connotation with them, referring to the doctrine Wesley called "Christian perfection," also known as "entire sanctification." The thought is that, upon accepting Jesus Christ, the believer is *justified* by God but that this is then the beginning of God's work of *sanctification,* namely, getting the believer's life and behavior transformed into that Christlikeness which is "holiness." Wesley's particular emphasis was that one dare not settle with that sanctification stopping anywhere short of "perfection." By "perfection," Wesley had in mind not so much "moral faultlessness" as "total acquiesence to the guidance and power of God"—though the one would seem necessarily to imply the other.

However, the important note is that Wesley never claimed that he was perfect nor did he encourage anyone else to claim so. In fact, it is more likely that he would have interpreted anyone's *claim* to be perfect as proof enough that he wasn't.

Wesley's concern, rather, seems to have been two-fold: (1) Because sanctification is God's work and not man's achievement, it would be blasphemous to declare the *impossibility* of its eventuating in perfection. (2) It would be a failure of faith in God for a believer to rest content with less than God's *full* intention for him. Yet, for the rest, as to *who* became perfect *when,* Wesley was willing to leave the matter in the hands of God where it belongs.

Although given a somewhat distinctive theological rationale, modern "holiness" seems to be as much as synonymous with what earlier had been called "pietism" (which see) and out of which tradition Wesley himself had come. It probably is not far wrong to think of the "holiness churches" as latter-day "pietists" who have adopted the *theological* base of contemporary "evangelicalism." To a real extent, their "holiness-piety" (focusing, as it does, on authenticity of *life* rather than correctness of *doctrine*) puts them into closer affinity with other "pietists" and with what we will call "sectaries" (see "Sect") than with establishment evangelicalism.

Both Wesley and the nineteenth-century progenitors of "holiness" understood sanctification as a deep-working, widely-effective leaven whose power can and does transform the communal life of the church and even of society. Thus, their faith included an active and effectual *social* concern. Yet, more recently, under the influence of an evangelicalism that tends to see sanctification as confined simply to the life of private moral virtue, there has been an erosion of this emphasis.

When true to their heritage, the "holiness churches" have a witness that needs to be more clearly spoken and more readily heard than has been the case within the body of Christ.

LIBERAL

Sprinkle Liberally

This treatment will need to be constructed with great care, because "liberal" is going to have to bear a great deal of weight—standing, as it does, as counterpart to "conservative," "evangelical," "fundamentalist," and "orthodox," all four.

We were just congratulating the alphabet for having given us the logical sequence of "evangelical" followed immediately by "fundamentalist." But we spoke too enthusiastically too soon; the order in this case is close but not close enough. "Liberal" would do better coming just *after* "orthodox" rather than just *before*. Indeed, I will be frank to admit that I jumped ahead and wrote "orthodox" to get a running start on "liberal." I would strongly advise the reader to fudge on alphabetical propriety in the same way. Regarding the theological spectrum we have been delineating, our suggestion is that "orthodox" be the broad term that comes clear up to the border of "liberal" and that—within "orthodoxy"—"conservative," "evangelical," and "fundamentalist" be seen as ranges farther to the right.

The word "liberal," of course, is used among us in a host of ways, some of them entirely secular and others (even in the church) entirely uncontroversial. For instance, all would agree that Christians are called to be *liberal* givers. Indeed, in this regard, conservatives, in general, may be more liberal than the liberals. However, don't be so rash as to tell a conservative that he is more liberal than the liberals unless you explain what you mean by that. With this, we make a primary point: the word "liberal" always needs supplementary explanation if communication is to take place.

"Liberal" (not over against "conservative" now) can denote an attitude of openness: the willingness to hear and consider all sorts of ideas, whether one agrees with them or not; the readiness to recognize and respect the integrity of people whose beliefs are quite different from one's own. And hear this: such an attitude has absolutely no correlation to liberal-conservative on the theological scale. It is true, of course, that we have as much as defined "fundamentalists" as being *illiberal* conservatives; but I know evangelicals who are as "liberal" of spirit as any Christian could be; and I know liberals who, in their own liberal theological views, are as dogmatic and narrow-minded as any fundamentalist. "Liberal," in this respect, is a Christian virtue that knows no theological particularity.

Now, as we finally turn to consider "liberal" in the theological sense, it must be observed that—as with "conservative"—the term performs best as a direct comparative between two clearly identified entities. And it can be used this way at any point on the spectrum. So, one might say, "Malcolm Muggeridge is more *liberal* than Francis Schaeffer"—even though neither of them can be called a *liberal*. So, again, it could be said, "The idea that the Bible is infallible in its central message is more *liberal* than the idea of its being infallible regarding every detail of which it speaks"—even though neither idea can be called a *liberal* one.

Even so (and probably "inevitably so"), the terms "liberal" and "conservative" also get used in an absolute sense, without any standard of comparison being stated. In such case, what standard is implied?

It is at this point, I feel, we often inject a complication that makes the matter even more difficult than it needs be. We confuse a non-theological definition of "liberal" with the theological one, assume that they necessarily go together, and proceed to judge someone a "liberal" on the one basis and then apply the term to him (falsely) on the other.

The non-theological measure is that of *methodology,* namely, *how* one goes about reading and interpreting the Scriptures; the theological one has to do with the *content* of faith (without regard as to whether it takes the form of direct biblical exposition or not).

"Liberal," regarding *methodology,* denotes a willingness to submit the biblical materials to those methods of analysis commonly called "higher criticism." We cannot take time to describe higher criticism in detail; but it is marked by the *willingness,* in the face of proper evidence, *to consider* such eventualities as these: that a book of the Bible may not have been written by the person to whom tradition (or even the text itself) assigns it; that certain passages could have been interpolated into a book by someone other than the author; that some statements ascribed to Jesus may represent the Gospel writer's idea of what Jesus would have been willing to say rather than a record of his literal words; that some scriptural statements reflect more of timebound cultural conditioning than they do of an inspired word from God.

On the other hand, "liberal," regarding *theology,* has reference to one's departure from Christian orthodoxy.

The potential discrepancy between these two measures of "liberalism" explains, I would suggest, the anomaly of Karl Barth (mentioned under "Evangelical"). When the older evangelicals called Barth a "liberal," they had in mind primarily his methodology, the fact that he was willing to desert a literalist, infallibilist view of the Scriptures in his use of higher criticism. (And this is a proper enough use of "liberal"—*if it had been made clear what they were saying by the term.*) Conversely, when some contemporary evangelicals want to recognize Barth as the author of *Evangelical Theology* and himself an evangelical, they are affirming that his thought falls well within the range of Christian orthodoxy. (And they, too, are correct: Barth would have had no difficulty at all with either the WCC statement—"[We] confess the Lord Jesus Christ as God and Savior according to the Scriptures"—or the New Testament kerygma [see the explanation under "Orthodox"].) Both the older evangelicals and the contemporaries are speaking true—if the frames of reference are kept straight.

But what must be insisted is that methodological liberalism need not necessarily—and does not normally—either involve or lead to theological liberalism. Granted, there have been attempts (more so in the past than now) to use higher-critical methodologies to refute the Bible or make it say something different from what orthodoxy has understood it to say; but these have been shown to be faulty uses—or sometimes deliberate misuses—of the method itself. The science of higher criticism, in itself, provides the one most effective rebuttal to those who would try to use it as a rationale for theological liberalism; for the one clearest, most widely accepted, and best established finding of so-called "liberal" biblical scholarship is that the Bible is an "orthodox" book.

(That last is, in one sense, a circular statement, because the reader will soon observe that we *define* orthodoxy in terms of the *biblical* kerygma. But what we are saying is that higher criticism has had the effect of giving scientific, scholarly support to the fact that orthodoxy's reading has in general been an accurate reading not only of the biblical texts but of the events that lie behind them.)

It is highly significant, for example, that the

discovery, identification, and establishing of the historicity of the orthodox, New Testament kerygma has been the work of methodologically "liberal" scholars and not "conservative" ones. Indeed, I think it irrefutable that the people who have been most effective in demonstrating that theological liberalism is not biblically derived and cannot claim a biblical basis are the methodologically liberal Bible scholars.

Yes, there are heterodox, theologically liberal thinkers among the higher critics; but there is no evidence that their methodological liberalism was a cause of the theological. Rather, theological liberalism normally shows itself as: (1) a reading of the Scriptures that higher criticism itself would refute; (2) a use of higher criticism that most scholars would brand as defective; (3) a doing of theology that doesn't even make a pretense of being biblical; or, as has happened, (4) a scholar's ignoring his own biblical findings when it comes to developing his theology.

Along with the above, consider that even the most conservative view on the literal infallibility of the Bible is itself no guarantee of theological orthodoxy; many of the groups that would have to be qualified as heterodox "cults" (which see) nevertheless claim a conservative doctrine of the Scriptures. What it comes to is that *being* biblical (*living* biblically) and holding a strict doctrine of inspiration are two entirely different things that don't even necessarily go together.

This applies not only at the boundary between orthodoxy and heterodoxy but *within* orthodoxy as well. For example, my own judgment regarding pop evangelicalism (see under "Evangelical") is that what we see there is a group of Christians holding a very high view of the Bible and yet acting most unbiblically. When it comes to the question as to which Christians are "being biblical," I doubt whether any distinction can be made between those methodologically liberal and those methodologically conservative.

Indeed, it could be argued (and I am volunteering to do so) that a *methodological* liberalism affords one a better chance of getting biblical than conservatism does. The net effect of higher-critical study (*good* higher-critical study, let it be said) is to sort things out so that the Bible can develop its own emphases, render its own judgments as to what of their truth is most vital and important. Thus is the concept "biblical" sharpened, focused, and underlined. But with a doctrine of total infallibility, any verse from whatever book of the Bible is just as "true," just as much "the inspired word of God," as any other. Not *inevitably,* perhaps, but very possibly this can have the effect of turning the believer free to find a text that will support whatever he chooses to believe or do— and have the support of the infallible word of God in the process.

But be that as it may, the point we truly are concerned to make is that, although the question of "liberal" or "conservative" methods of biblical interpretation is an important one, it does not mark the boundary between orthodoxy and heterodoxy, and it ought not be made the litmus test for identifying a "liberal" in the absolutist sense.

Granted, then, that within Christian orthodoxy there are those whose method of approaching the Scriptures is more "liberal" than "conservative" and that, even theologically, some are more "liberal" than others; nevertheless, we are proposing that anyone in this group not be called a "liberal" unless the term is used as a direct comparative with the frame of reference clearly indicated. A "liberal" in the absolute sense, then, would be reserved to designate those of heterodox theology, whose theological position puts them outside of Christian orthodoxy (measured, we are suggesting, by the WCC statement and/or the New Testament kerygma). But where does such "liberalism" come from, and how does it make itself apparent?

I am ready to suggest that, almost invariably, "liberalism" begins its defection by taking a different from orthodox view of Man, his situation and the course of his history. When orthodox affirmations call Jesus "Savior," the clear and inescapable implication is that Man—although created good—has broken his relationship to God and deserted God's intention for him in such wise that he has become, if not absolutely evil, at least headed determinedly in the wrong direction. This direction is away from his true humanity and toward death and destruction. Indeed, so dogged is Man's go-it-alone wrongheadedness that only a "Savior"—an intervention of that which is outside of and different from "humanity"—gives any chance of getting things turned around.

Liberalism regularly denies that any turn-around of so radical a nature is needed; and from this heterodox premise, heterodox implications begin to emerge. It is important at this point to realize that "liberalism" does not identify any one particular theological position. Some liberals draw some of the conclusions listed below; others draw others. It is unfair to treat liberals as though they are all alike, accusing them all of believing what those "farthest out" do.

Yet there are implications that begin to follow: (1) The course of human history marks the *ascent* of Man. Some see this as a hard-fought struggle involving plateaus and reversals; others see it as being as natural and regular as a baby's growing into adulthood. Yet, either way, the innate character of human history is *progress*.

(2) The combination of Man's cognitive, rational, intuitive, and aesthetic powers comprise the potential for his discovering the ultimate truth about life, himself, and the universe; and the progress of history is measured precisely as growth in this understanding.

(3) It follows that contemporary wisdom marks the highest point yet in this development. Therefore, whatever truth there may be in the Scriptures is to be tried against the standard of our modern, culturally-acquired insight rather than vice versa. Revelation (even if understood as coming from God) is the process of Man's gradual ascent into truth. There is, then, no need for God to

have made a unique and essential revelation to one special people, at one special time, through one special event in history—and it is inconceivable that he did so. Thus, although many if not most Christian liberals still find the Bible a source of true and helpful teachings, I think one of the surest indicators is that they take "what modern man knows" rather than "the New Testament kerygma" as being the norm of Truth.

(4) Although Jesus may be recognized as a great teacher and even as *the* person who best represents the goal toward which Man is evolving, he cannot strictly be called "Savior"—because Man has no need of the radical turnaround that term would suggest. Jesus, at most, is a firstfruit—both product and promise—of Man's own development.

(5) An intervention by God that would *change* the course of Man's history is, of course, neither wanted nor called for. God *can* be the one who encourages, nurtures, and applauds the maturation of Man. Or he *can* be a name designating the world-process itself, or the principle behind it. Or he *can* be an "idea" that was helpful in earlier stages of Man's development but which now can be dispensed with.

Liberalism, of course, can take the form of a sheerly secular philosophy that neither wants nor claims any relationship to Christianity; but how far along the above line of thought can the ideas be called "Christian" or the people who hold them be called "Christians"?

That's a hard one. The name of the faith deliberately is *"Christ*ianity" rather than *"Jesus*anity." "Christ" means "the Messiah, the Chosen One, the Anointed of God"—which, applied to Jesus, carries very strong overtones of "Savior," the One through whom the natural course of Man is dramatically reversed. In short, "Christ" is a word that unavoidably implies orthodoxy and has accuracy only within the framework of orthodoxy. Nevertheless, theologians who are members, teachers, and/or ministers within denominations, the official statements and vows of which are strictly orthodox, hold positions running clear through No. 5 above; and they still call their theology and themselves "Christian." In practice, apparently, we are willing to use the term "Christianity" in relation to any and all thought that grants some sort of recognition and deference to the man Jesus.

Now if I had my own "druthers," I would insist that we use the term more precisely, as a designation of Christian orthodoxy; and I say that, not from any desire to put down or cast out anyone, but simply to enable the language to do the work language is designed to do. So when the choice is mine and I get to use the word my way, "Christianity" means orthodoxy, i.e., thought or action based upon the premises of the New Testament kerygma. Yet, at the same time, I am not going to try to stop other people from using the term as they choose to use it—which means that I will have to listen carefully in detecting how they *are* using it. Then too, rather than arguing, I am willing to call another person whatever he wants to be called—even if it is my private opinion that he is stretching the blanket farther than it will cover.

Even so, it is interesting to observe that, on their own, liberals often betray an ambiguity toward the word "Christianity." Even while maintaining membership and/or ordination in a Christian church and presumably thinking of themselves as Christians, they have an uneasiness about the particularity of the word and so tend to go to the term "religion." "Religion," of course, can refer to almost anything, all the efforts Man has made and does make to establish the higher values of life and orient himself toward them—and there is no question but that liberalism qualifies under such a definition. But when the big word becomes "religion," scratch the speaker, and you are almost certain to find a liberal.

"Liberalism" itself, of course, covers a wide enough variety of theological thought that we very often will need to be able to make distinctions within it. Perhaps "moderate" and "ultraliberal" would do in distinguishing between those who do strive to think in biblical terms and maintain a connection with biblical thought (although obviously not centering upon the kerygma) and those who do theology entirely in terms of the wisdom of the modern world. However, the move I most adamantly resist (for reasons explained elsewhere) is to label the ultraliberals as "radical" (which see).

LITURGICAL

Up-Sa-Daisy!

"Liturgical," thank goodness, does not have to do with the theological spectrum with which we have been wrestling; its complications are of a different sort. The word "liturgy" is used in reference to the rites and activities a group goes through in the course of its public worship; so every church has a liturgical tradition of one sort or another.

However, the word itself is very interesting, being one that has done a complete somersault of meaning in the course of its development. It is constructed out of two Greek words meaning "laity" and "work"; logically, then, it would refer to "the part played by the laity in a Sunday morning service" (or something to that effect). Yet, in time, the word began to point more toward "the worship activity done for the edification of the laity" and finally came to designate "the *priest's* work."

Now, to speak of a "liturgical church" is not to refer to every and any church—although each does have its liturgical practice. Neither does it (as the etymology of the term should signify) refer to those where the service proceeds: "Who has a hymn they'd like to sing this morning?" "Let us now have a period of testimonies from the congregation." "Brother Jones, would you lead us in prayer?" Quite the contrary, the less initiative the laity has, the more "liturgical" a church it is. "Liturgical," then, identifies the degree of *formality* in a church's worship tradition. Vestments, candles, symbols and paraphernalia, set prayers, prescribed formulas and movements—these are the things that make a church "liturgical." And this sort of liturgy, of course, centers in the "churches" (see "Churchly") and is one element in the overall pattern we call "churchliness." The Roman Catholic, Eastern Orthodox, Anglican, and Lutheran churches are prime examples.

In order to handle this phenomenon comparatively, there came into the language the terms "high-church" and "low-church." They first were used within a single denomination to distinguish those *congregations* that were more liturgical from those that were less so. However, the comparison becomes all the more striking when applied across denominational lines. One of the most visible and natural—although by no means most basic— distinctions between the "churches" and the "sects" (which see) is that, liturgically, the churches are high-church and the sects low.

Interestingly, in our day, we may be seeing the birth of a third liturgical type that is neither "high" nor "low"; it will require a new category. What I have in mind is described under "pop

evangelicalism" (see "Evangelical"). Its prac-
titioners come, for the most part, out of low-
church traditions; and their liturgy doesn't rate for
much by any accepted liturgical norms. Yet there
is an all-out effort to bring the program off with
"class," having the whole professionally engineered
and orchestrated (so it will be "right" for the TV
cameras). The norms are those of show business
rather than ecclesiastical tradition.

Because we already have high-church and low-
church, perhaps this one could be called "chic-
church" (and its liturgy, "chic-lit"). Indeed, we
could even speak of "high-chic" and "low-chic."
High-chic emulates a Lawrence Welk mode: "See
and hear a choir of a thousand voices massed
behind seven musical fountains as soloist Glamora
Starr, straight from her latest Broadway musical,
sings *Jesus Paid It All*. An offering will be taken."
Low-chic emulates more the style of the Grand Ol'
Opry: "As the climax of his sermon The Reverend
Billy Lane will set hisself afire in order to give
sinners a small hint of what all is in store for them.
It will pay you to be there. An offering will be
taken."

LOW CHURCH (see Liturgical)

MILLENARIAN / MILLENNIALIST
(see Fundamentalist)

MODERNIST (see Fundamentalist)

ORTHODOX

The Broad One

In dealing with the theological spectrum of Christendom, we have had difficulty finding a term which can be used over against "liberal" so as to divide the entire field between them. "Conservative" (which see) won't do; there are too many Christians in the center who are more conservative than the liberals but also more liberal than the conservatives and who, thus, cannot accurately be labeled either way.

"Evangelical" (which see) is even worse. There has been some tendency of late for the evangelical movement to expand toward the left and *claim* all who are not liberals. This, for instance, is the case with Karl Barth who, during his lifetime, was, by the evangelicals, branded as a "liberal" but now, by the sons of those evangelicals, is being claimed as an "evangelical." But "evangelical" is actually so closely identified with a particular historio-cultural complex that this move is a clear case of hegemony, one state's dominating and trying to absorb another.

"Orthodox," then, is the term now suggested as being broad enough and uncolored enough to cover both the right *and center* clear up to the borders of liberalism—even though this usage will not be without its problems.

The least of these is the fact that a number of church bodies include the word "orthodox" in their titles and, together, are known as the "Eastern Orthodox" churches. These are national churches of the area that once constituted the Eastern, or Byzantine, Empire as over against the Western Empire centered at Rome. Division along this line was implicit within Christendom from early in its history; but it is since A.D. 1054 that the Orthodox churches have been completely independent from the Catholicism of the West.

The Orthodox churches are invariably "churchly" (which see) and highly "liturgical" (which see). Their theological teaching also is "orthodox" in the sense we will now proceed to use the term— although our usage has no special reference to those churches.

The word "orthodox" is derived from two words, the first meaning "right, or correct," the second meaning "thought, or opinion." It can, of course, be used in many different connections, both religious and secular; we are considering it only in regard to Christian theology. Also, quite evidently, it can be used in either a broad or narrow way. Particularly as one moves to the right, farther into conservatism, the tendency will be to define "orthodox" more and more narrowly; almost by definition, fundamentalists will see themselves as the only orthodox believers.

Our plea is that the constrictive impulse be resisted and the term "orthodox" be kept relatively open and inclusive. There is good precedent for doing so; within recent memory we witnessed a theological movement (of which Karl Barth was the most notable representative) called "Neo-Orthodoxy," i.e., "the new orthodoxy"—and that in itself would signify the inclusion of a great many Christians who ought not to be called either "evangelicals" or "conservatives."

To be "orthodox," then, is to stand theologically within the general, historically-recognized tradition of the Christian faith.

But how is that faith to be defined? To do it too broadly is to lose the concept "orthodox" (*correct* opinion) entirely; to do it too narrowly is to exclude some who truly are within the tradition. Obviously, we will need to spot some general limits and parameters but also avoid all attempts to draw any strict definition. For a starter, we might suggest a widely recognized, *modern* statement, the basis of membership of the World Council of Churches, already subscribed to by more than 286 different denominations. (And it is plain, regarding the more conservative churches who have declined to join, that it is not because of any unwillingness to affirm the following statement:) "[We] confess the Lord Jesus Christ as God and Savior according to the Scriptures and therefore seek to fulfill together [our] common calling to the glory of the one God, Father, Son, and Holy Spirit."

It is safe to say, I think, that, in their official teachings, the churches that have made this affirmation—plus many conservative churches that have not—all fall within what we are proposing to call "Christian orthodoxy." Yet, at the same time, it must be recognized that a number of these denominations include individual thinkers (and non-thinking members) whose personal theology would not qualify. This definition, then, does exclude non-WCC liberal churches (see "Liberal"), liberals within member denominations, and the cults (which see) as being outside of Christian orthodoxy.

There is another way of coming at our definition (which, I think, would end up having about the same people in and out). Obviously, the entire tradition of Christian orthodoxy takes its source from and is based upon the New Testament; the New Testament is itself the original expression of that faith. And in our day, through methods of very careful analysis and weighing of the biblical evidence, scholars have come to a general consensus regarding what they call the *kerygma*. "Kerygma" is the New Testament Greek word signifying "proclamation, or preached message"; and it is, then, that pattern of beliefs which the early church saw as being the core of its witness, the ideas it stressed as being basic and essential to Christian belief. Other teachings, of course, follow from these; but the kerygma is the seed from which everything else springs.

Different scholars, of course, will vary the wording; but Reginald Fuller's statement would win general consent:

> Jesus of Nazareth,
> born of the seed of David,
> died,
> was buried:
> God raised him the third day
> and exalted him to his right hand
> as Messiah, Lord, and Son of God
> until he comes as Judge and Savior.
> In all this God has fulfilled his promises in Scripture
> and inaugurated the Age to Come.
> The apostles are witnesses of these things,
> and offer to those who accept their message
> baptism for remission of sins
> and the gift of the Holy Spirit.

Without arguing about details of wording or the literal meaning of each phrase, the general thrust of this kerygma would seem to make a good litmus test as to whether a given theology represents Christian orthodoxy or not.

Once we have "orthodox" in hand, there are some related words that will help flesh out the concept. "Unorthodox," "heterodox," and "heretical" should be used with clearly distinguished meanings.

"Unorthodox," we suggest, should designate

belief or practice that varies from the majority opinion within orthodoxy but does in no sense mark a move away from the basic definition of orthodoxy itself. Thus, for example, the entire concept of church membership implied by the believers' church (which see) was most *unorthodox* when introduced into Christendom. Just so is the attitude the sects (which see) have taken toward the churches (see "Churchly") and toward society in general. Just so, again, is the interpretation of the gospel that forbids participation in war. Yet, in none of these cases is there any question of a changed relationship to the theological orthodoxy of the kerygma. Christian orthodoxy is such as to allow for some very unorthodox churches—of which I am proud to belong to one.

The case is quite otherwise with "heterodox"; it identifies "a *different* opinion"—and that precisely on the matters that *define* orthodoxy. A heterodox theology, then, is one that either denies essential elements of orthodoxy or imports alien ideas into it. A theology of "the death of God," for example, rather clearly is heterodox; its proponents inevitably would have trouble with either the WCC statement or the New Testament kerygma.

It is one thing, of course, for a person to practice or preach an honest heterodoxy, that is, frankly and openly admit that he has rejected Christian orthodoxy in favor of different beliefs and interpretations (even if he still chooses to call them "Christian" in some sense of his own). However, it is quite another thing for a person to try to pass off heterodox doctrine *as being* orthodoxy, to call kerygma that which is not kerygma, to make "the faith once delivered" something other than that which was once delivered. And it is only in connection with this second phenomenon that it would seem proper to use the words "heresy" and "heretical." There is a world of difference between a teaching with which I happen to disagree and which I consider to be wrong as over against one that is presented under false pretenses. "Heresy" is a serious word and one that ought to be used only with great seriousness and discrimination within the body of Christ. It certainly ought not be used (though it often has been) in regard to simple "unorthodoxy" and, I would say, not even in regard to "honest heterodoxy."

PENTECOSTAL (see Charismatic)

PIETIST

The Goody-Goodies

"Pietism" carries both a specific meaning and a general one. The two tend to get confused with each other but ought not. The second really ought to be dropped but probably won't be. We begin with the first.

"Pietism," in the specific sense, refers to a revival movement within the Christian church which can be rather clearly traced historically and rather closely characterized as to its nature. It arose within Continental Protestantism (Germany and the Low Countries) in the late seventeenth century, spread and crested during the eighteenth century, and continues to flow right into the present.

It began as a protest against the cold formalism and intellectual scholasticism of the "churches" (see "Churchly") and as an attempt to revive them. Yet even while working revival from within, Pietism also was giving birth to groupings of its own: the Brethren family (the Church of the Brethren and its siblings); the Renewed Moravian Church; Wesleyan Methodism and its later spin-offs, the Holiness Churches (which see) and the Salvation Army; plus any number of short-lived cults (which see).

The central thrust of Pietism is that true Christianity always must be life- and experience-centered rather than centered either in theology (doctrine, creed) or in liturgy. The crucial question, then, is not "Do you hold the correct beliefs about and go through the correct motions in the worship of Jesus?" but "Do you truly *love* Jesus, and have you truly experienced his presence in your heart?" Pietism, inevitably, includes a strong *experiential* component with overtones of feeling, warmth, and openings of the heart.

Even so (and we here make the point that is absolutely crucial to our discussion), from this experiential center there immediately follows an idea that is so inevitable that it must be given equal consideration as an essential component in the true Pietism of which we speak. The implication is this: if a person's "experience" of Jesus is genuine, it necessarily will bear fruit in his outward conduct and particularly in his concern for his fellowmen.

One of the earliest Pietist leaders (Francke) was a founder of schools and orphanages. The modern foreign-mission program of the Protestant church was founded out of Pietist circles. The German Pietist churches (Church of the Brethren and Moravian) always have shown notable social awareness. John Wesley was a leader of social reforms affecting the poorer classes in England. At the time of their origins in the nineteenth century, the holiness churches were active in opposing slavery and in recognizing the equality of women. The Salvation Army was born out of Pietist influences. It can be demonstrated that the quality of Christian social concern that characterizes so much of Christendom today is in large degree an inheritance from the Pietist movement. From the beginning, this was an essential component of what it means to be "Pietist."

It should be noted here that Pietism has much in common with the earlier movement of "Anabaptism" (which see); it is a congruence with a difference of emphasis. Pietism centers on the personal experience of "love for Jesus" and then moves to an *"obedience* to Jesus" which is something like radical discipleship (though perhaps less "radical" for being in second place). Anabaptism, conversely, seems to center upon "obedience to Jesus" (radical discipleship) without denying the need of the experiential "love for Jesus." Anabaptism has been stronger on discipleship and restoration of the New Testament church order (believers' baptism, etc.) and weaker on feeling, warmth, and openings of the heart. Pietism has been stronger on inner experience but perhaps not as strongly concerned about New Testament discipleship (thus, for example, many of the Pietist groups practice infant baptism even while holding pretty much a believers'-baptism concept of the church).

The Church of the Brethren marks precisely an

historical intersection of original Pietism (1708) and the older Anabaptist tradition with which its Pietist founders had come in contact. Consequently, it became a dialectical effort at working out of a double center, giving "obedience to Jesus" and "love for Jesus" equal and simultaneous attention. It's a neat trick which we cannot brag about having pulled off with complete success.

From its beginnings, of course, Pietism had to bear the opposition of the "churches" whose ways it was protesting. The opponents did their job by giving the very term "Pietist" a twist, picking up one of Pietism's truths and ignoring the other in order to produce a half-truth. A "pietist" now (note the small "p") became "a goody-goody," i.e., any Christian whose sole interest was in having himself a thrilling inner experience, getting himself pious, making himself good and virtuous and nice in God's eyes, saving himself through his piety.

Now, undoubtedly there are and always have been "pietists" of this stripe. But the "Pietists"— with their essential emphasis on sanctification and fruitbearing—were never the "pietists" (if we may put it so); and it was nothing but slanderous deliberately to manipulate the terminology to hang them with the charge. Yet that has now been done for so long that the word "pietist" undoubtedly will continue to be used in a general sense identifying self-centered goody-goodies. The best we can do at this point is to separate the two usages, making it very clear when we are referring to the historical movement and its contemporary manifestations and when we are referring to a privatized, moralistic version of Christianity.

How complex that double usage is bound to become is made apparent when we relate Pietism to the modern movement we have called "evangelicalism" (see "Evangelical"). In this century, some of the Pietist groups (for example, the holiness churches) have tended to merge into evangelicalism; others (for example, the Church of the Brethren) have not. In any case, there are some Pietists and some Pietistic influences within evangelicalism. Yet the evangelical tradition itself, as a whole, cannot be called Pietistic; its more central emphases have been (1) correct doctrine and (2) inner experience—but with a noticeable slighting of Pietism's "first implication" regarding the fruits of social concern and service. Consequently, there tends to be more of "pietism" (small "p" now) within evangelicalism and fundamentalism than in any other sector of the church. Thus, to put the matter most maddeningly, Pietists need to take care that evangelicalism does not corrupt their Pietism with pietism.

RADICAL

The Radius of a Radish

"Radical" is a very good, helpful, and meaningful word which modern usage (misusage) has as much as *ruined* for all practical purposes.

The word, of course, is used in secular as well as Christian contexts; but this is not the source of the difficulty. No, that seats in the "root" meaning of the word itself. "Radical"—along with "radius," "radish," and more than a dictionary page of other terms—is built on the Latin root that means "root." Thus, the "radius" is a line that goes to the center, the root, of a circle. A radish is a "radish," because what we eat is the *root* of the plant. And thus, by rights, "radical" ought to identify thought or action that gets to the *root* of the matter at hand, that drives most profoundly to the fundamental source. (Amusing as it must seem, if fundamentalists were truly "fundamental" and radicals were truly "radical," they would both be at the same place; etymologically, the two words are virtually synonymous. But unfortunately, the

106

name of a group often has no necessary relationship to its reality.)

Yet, in general, we tend to use the word "radical" in identifying twigs rather than roots, that which is farthest out rather than closest in, that which is the latest thing rather than the original, that which is pushing toward extremism rather than rootage. Those who call themselves radicals and whom we recognize as radicals most often are the ultraliberals who see themselves as avant garde, out in front, leaving the old behind— and thus the people farthest from having any interest in recovering a heritage or repristinating an historical revelation.

Still, even with this reversal, there is a sense in which these radicals accurately can be related to the "roots," although we will contend that to do so only confuses the matter further. Now these people are "radical" in the sense that they are questioning the establishment *at its roots,* shaking the foundations; what they pose is a fundamental, a *root,* challenge.

It is true that any authentic "radicalism" will have the effect of upsetting the establishment and calling it into question. It is plain, for example, that Jesus' ministry had this effect upon the Jewish establishment he confronted. Nevertheless, "radicalism" cannot be located and defined simply by this negative effect, because the truth of the matter is that wind in the twigs will shake the establishment bole just as much as will a tremor of the rooted ground. Not the negative effect of the shaking but the positive intention of outcome must be the measure of true radicalism. Thus, what made Jesus truly "radical" was not simply his root-challenge of the establishment; it was the fact that he was calling for a "conversion," a turning back to the truth of Israel's origins—this, rather than willing the destruction of the establishment so that he might introduce some innovative conception of his own.

Properly used, it should be evident, "radical" is a term that would be a natural in dealing with the Christian gospel and the relationship of different Christians and groups to it. But we have not used—nor are we using—the term properly. We use it with twigs rather than roots. Thus, "radical theology" is the accepted designation for the God-is-dead persuasion and related viewpoints, when there is no possible way of arguing that they mark a move toward what could be called the *roots* of Christianity.

There is in circulation a journal entitled *Radical Religion*; and in this case, the choice of the word "religion" seems to betray precisely the significance we proposed earlier (see under "Liberal"), namely, a hesitancy about being committed to the theology of Christian orthodoxy. The contents of the journal would suggest that the "radical" of the title means only "joining the parade of causes that the socio-political world calls 'radical,'" for the treatments show virtually no interest in biblical, theological, kerygmatic rootage. "Radical," here, cannot mean what it Christianly ought to mean; and, failing to identify what roots we could be talking about, the word communicates

very little at all. Indeed, "religion" is such a
general and all-inclusive term to begin with that I
am hard put to think what its "roots" or "a turn to
its roots" might be.

What has happened, I think, (of which the
above is just one illustration) is that, rather than
giving "radical" its proper *Christian* sense, we have
simply imported it into the Christian vocabulary
while letting it continue to carry the secular, socio-
political overtones of the world. It is not within
our purview here to try to say what "radical"
ought to mean *politically,* to specify what root
system is there in mind. But when the political
term is imported into Christianity, what it *does*
become, I am convinced, is an identification of
those believers who, in pursuit of their Christian
social concerns, are willing to use the techniques
and means that politically are called "radical."

What this amounts to, in our day, is that the
Christians most commonly tagged as radicals are
those who are so opposed to establishment oppres-
sion and violence that they are willing to support
(or at least countenance) revolutionary manipulation and violence as a counterforce. Now, whether
or not this qualifies as a good definition of
political radicalism, I don't know; but it can't
begin to qualify as *Christian* radicalism. Begin,
biblically, to trace the Christian rootage in this
matter and it becomes clear that the Christian is to
eschew violence and manipulation *totally.* He can
afford to do this, because he sees fundamental
social change as depending upon the resurrection-
power of God rather than upon what will have to

be brought about by that which *human* means can achieve. The Christian's way is neither that of the establishment nor of the revolution but that of the *cross,* i.e., defenseless love and voluntary subordination.

Obviously, the supporter of establishment violence is not being radically Christian; his is ⸌ way of the world, and he's in the wrong root system. But just as obviously, the supporter of revolutionary violence is not being *radically* Christian either; his, too, is a way of the world; and although he may be doing a better job of *political* root-seeking than the establishment supporter is, he still is in the same root system with him—and it's not the Christian one.

So it all adds up to the fact that the word "radical" has been as much as ruined for any useful purpose in the Christian vocabulary; too many false meanings have become attached to it. Yet we dare not let the word go completely; potentially, it has too much utility and value. But what this means is that the word cannot be used by itself, in any absolutist sense ("He is a radical.") No, "radical" must become an adjective to some noun that specifies the root system in mind.

"Radical Christianity" is a term that now has some currency. This is helpful and should have the effect of limiting the definition so as to avoid a lot of the misunderstanding. Nevertheless, the term "Christianity" is itself broad enough that one gets little inkling as to what the speaker sees as the specific focus of the radicality, what "roots" he has in mind. For instance, the fundamentalist's doctrine of the inspiration of the Scriptures could conceivably be called a "radical" one; and on that basis he might (although he is not likely to) claim his as being "radical Christianity." The difficulty is that neither the kerygma, the New Testament as a whole, nor the early Christian tradition can be made to support the idea that a particular doctrine of inspiration ever was used as a test of faith or considered a fundamental root of the faith.

(It can be said that all the measuring rods of Christian orthodoxy *do* clearly emphasize the necessity of accepting the biblical *message* as true and reliable; this, then, *is* a root, a tap root even. Anything qualifying as *radical* Christianity will *have* to be strongly biblical. But that is not to say that it has to center on a particular doctrine of inspiration. As was observed earlier, *being* biblical and holding a strict doctrine of inspiration are two quite different things.)

Or again, the charismatics could be understood to hold a "radical" view regarding glossolalia and on that basis claim to represent "radical Christianity." But again, the difficulty is that none of the tests can be made to demonstrate that tongue-speaking ever was considered a central root of what "Christianity" means. As a term, then, "radical *Christianity*" simply is not specific enough to communicate precisely what one means by the adjective *"radical."*

Perhaps the noun that will best fit and protect the adjective "radical" is "discipleship." "Radical discipleship" is rapidly establishing itself as a term in the Christian vocabulary; and it does get the roots set right.

"Discipleship" (the German *Nachfolge*) signifies a "following after Jesus." The "Jesus" it intends is the one named and designated in the kerygma (see under "Orthodox") and not some great ethical teacher, humanist hero, or anyone else. It is his title "Lord" that calls for discipleship and the fact that he has "inaugurated the Age to Come" that enables it. Furthermore, a radical "*following after* Jesus" necessarily implies a radical "*faith in* Jesus"; only a radical faith is sufficient motivation for a truly radical following (otherwise one would sink when called to walk on water).

"Radical discipleship," then, is the totally committed, root-probing effort—through Bible study, the spiritual disciplines, and the help of the Holy Spirit—to be made just as obedient to the Lord Jesus as it is possible to become. And once it is hooked to the word "discipleship," "radical" takes on definition and content to become a means of communicating, of describing and measuring, a real and rooted aspect of the gospel.

RELIGION (see Liberal)

SECT

The Church's Sect Appeal

The word "sect" is based, ultimately, upon an old Latin verb form meaning "to follow." Thus it *could* relate to the sort of radical discipleship, i.e., "following after Jesus," we just discussed under "Radical." However, this is not the derivation the term normally has been attributed. On the contrary, this might well be the one of our terms about which there has been the greatest confusion and which most deliberately has been used to divide the body of Christ.

"Sect," of course, can be used in an entirely non-ecclesiastical, non-Christian sense; but that need not concern us here. Also, it is used in an ecclesiastical but very broad and unperjorative sense (particularly in legal parlance) as identifying *any* particular grouping within the totality of the church. In this sense, any denomination is just as much a "sect" as any other; and thus the word "nonsectarian" inevitably denotes an activity or agency that cuts across all denominational lines. About this usage, again, there is nothing in particular that needs to be said.

Where the trouble arises is with the usage that identifies some denominations as being "small and different." However, the difficulty lies, not with this definition in and of itself (in fact, we shall see that it constitutes a very good place from which to start the defining process), but with the implications the judgment regularly carries; "small and different" is taken to read "narrow-minded, divisive, and wrong." Now there are, of course, groups that do display these latter characteristics; but such accusation must be made on a basis of supporting evidence, not simply as the obvious concomitant of their being small and different. Indeed, these accusers overlook the fact that their stricture hits the early Christian church—which was nothing if not small and different—as much as it does any other group they would belittle as a "sect."

Recently I heard an eminent church historian say that he defines a "sect" as a group that claims to hold the only true faith. Yet he is not consistent. If one were to make an honest examination of track records, the group in this regard that has been the most insistent over the longest period of time is the biggest of them all, the Roman Catholic Church. Much the same is true of other of the "churches" as well; in fact, it is invariably the "churches" and not the "sects" that actually have gone to war with one another over who represents the "true" faith.

Still, in the eyes of many, the very fact that a

"sect" (a *small* group) argues its right to an independent existence is taken as equivalent to a claim of its being the only true church. Yet that conclusion does not follow at all—and no one even thinks of applying the principle to large groups, who are just as adamant regarding *their* independent existences. If dogmatism and narrow-mindedness is the test, large groupings are just as capable of those traits as small ones are.

Be that as it may, the charge that really gets hung on the "sects" is *divisiveness*; "sectarian" comes to mean "divisive"; the sects are the ones responsible for fragmenting the body of Christ. But again, this is to read implications into "small and different" that don't necessarily follow at all. No one calls the Lutheran Church divisive for breaking off from Catholicism. What it comes to is that *big* divisions are proper—only small ones are criticized. (And by the way, Jesus and the apostles are the most divisive of all for pulling a handful of people out of Judaism to form their own sect.)

Also, it should be understood that the question of *truth* must be considered before *divisiveness* can be located at all (see under "Ecumenical"). Who is to say that when a small group is separated out from a large group it is inevitably the small group that is being divisive? It could be that the large group *forced* the small group out. Or, if the small group actually is the one closer to Christian truth, then the larger group is responsible for the divisiveness in refusing to be open to that truth. This is not to say that the "churches" have been responsible for all divisiveness and the "sects" for none. It is to say that divisiveness is a disease which knows nothing of a limit named "small and different." Regarding ecumenicity, the churches and the sects have about the same record: some good marks and some bad.

Finally, when the focus is on the "different" (of "small and different") another grave injustice is done to the "sects." The assumption automatically is made that "different" *must* mean "heterodox"— when plainly there is every possibility that it means simply "unorthodox" (see under "Orthodox" for this important distinction). Our terminology has been set up precisely to care for the eventuality. We propose that "cult" (which see), by definition, be used to identify *heterodox* groups and that "sect," by definition, be reserved for *unorthodox* groups within orthodoxy.

"Sects" by nature, then, are unorthodox; but we need to be more specific regarding the motive and direction of that unorthodoxy. They are unorthodox in their desire to pursue *a more radical discipleship* than that of the churchly establishment (and what we have said about this discipleship under "Radical" should here become a part of the discussion). We are not implying any judgment about how *true* any particular sect's understanding of discipleship may be or how successful it is in living it out; but we are spotting the *intention* that is central to the definition we are now ready to propose:

A "sect" is a minority, dissenting, although orthodox, Christian denomination which, through its desire to practice radical discipleship, finds itself in tension both with established Christendom and with secular society.

A sect, it follows from this definition, may be good or bad, on the mark or way off it; but that is a judgment which will have to be made sect by sect; it will not do simply to make sweeping accusations and put them down *as a category*. To do so is to buy into the idea that the majority is inevitably right, that "fifty million Frenchmen can't be wrong," or that any group that is "small and different" *must* be wrong. Now there may be areas of human experience in which this principle has some validity; but Christianity, for sure, is not one of them. Based upon an historical revelation of God, its truth always will have to be measured against that revelation; and any sort of opinion poll is entirely irrelevant.

In point of fact, there has been a sectarian strain running through Christian history from the beginning. As we have suggested, the church itself started as a Jewish sect. In Acts 24:5, Paul is called "a ringleader of the sect of the Nazarenes"; and in Acts 28:22, the Jews of Rome greet the apostle with these words: "We should like to hear from you what your views are; all we know about this sect is that no one has a good word to say for it." ("Small and different" groups never have had an easy time of it.)

After Constantine, then, when Christianity became itself an established, state-supported "church," sectarian groups made their appearance *within* Christianity. Roughly the line runs Montanism, Novatianism, Donatism, the Cluniac and Cistercian monastic reforms, Franciscanism, Waldensianism, the Anabaptists (and to a lesser extent, all the believers' churches), Pietism. In our own day, the new evangelicals (see "Evangelical") clearly represent a sectarian protest developing out of evangelicalism. (The only question in their case is whether people out of earlier sect-traditions ought simply be taken over and called "evangelicals.")

A couple of things, however, should now be clear. (1) "Sect" does not correlate neatly with any one range of the *theological* spectrum we have been developing. Sectarianism, with its radical discipleship, does belong within the broad range we have called Christian orthodoxy; but it can and does appear at any place within that range. Evangelicalism is *not*, in and of itself, sectarian; indeed, the current protest is directed against both what we have called the evangelical establishment and pop evangelicalism.

(2) We are not suggesting that all of Christian orthodoxy can be divided between "churches" and "sects." The "churches" we have defined as descendants of the tradition of territorial establishments supported by state and society. But it must be recognized that there are also among us many denominations which, although not coming out of that tradition, have been enculturated and have made their peace with the world in other ways, to the point that they show nothing of what could be called radical sectarian tension or dissent.

ZWINGLIAN

The Last Shall Be Last

Actually, there is no reason the contemporary Christian vocabulary needs the word "Zwinglian." It is included here only as a way of getting us to the end of the alphabet and an appropriate conclusion for this book. "Zwinglian" *is* the last theological term in the dictionary.

"Zwinglians" are the followers of Huldreich Zwingli of Zurich, Zwitzerland (1484-1531). In addition to being a person who worked hard at bringing up the alphabetical rear, he was the Protestant reformer whose most distinctive idea was that the Lord's Supper, rather than being a sacrament that somehow involved a real transmission of Christ's body and blood, is a meal by which Christians keep fresh the memory of what Christ did for them in the past and thus make themselves open to his approach and call in the present.

His view gained support—including, we would suggest, that of the New Testament. Today, a great number of churches and Christians could, on this

119

grounds, properly be called Zwinglians. However, few would appreciate the label and even fewer would understand what it meant. Our best move, then, is to leave Zwingli of Zurich in his alphabetical place as the final footnote at the end of the last page.

However, regarding "Zwinglian"—as regarding every other term treated in this book—take note that the author has let his personal bias show through. But that's all right. In the introduction of the book I promised that such would be the case, and I've kept my promise. So give me credit for that much, at least.

The very first person to read my manuscript, in making what will forever have to stand as the very first response to the book, opined that it probably never would be read by anyone who wouldn't get offended at one point or another. That may not be the most encouraging word an author has heard; but there is no help for it. Indeed, it only goes to show what is in truth the state of affairs within the body of Christ. There are differences of viewpoint which make it inevitable that some Christians are a cause of offense to other Christians.

I have been as frank and honest and forthright about these as I know how to be. And the book itself is meant as a proposal that it is precisely through such a stance—rather than through any sort of cover up, glossing over, or feigned fellowship—that the body has any chance of fully growing up into the head which is Christ. We have worked at making our vocabulary more useful to that purpose—and in the process I have had my say. That itself is an invitation for the reader to have his. Correct me where I'm wrong; correct yourself where you are; and let us use our vocabulary for an "in-body" dialog that will serve for the Lord's correcting us all.